Turtles As Pets.

Guide to keeping turtles.

Turtles diet, care, health, costs and feeding.

By

Digby Warren

Table of Contents

Introduction

If you're considering adding a turtle to your family or are just bringing one home for the first time, this guide has the information you will need to help you and your pet start off on the right foot with tips on how to house, care and feed your new friend.

Three questions that come to mind when deciding on a turtle would be why not just buy whichever one 'looks' good? Why do we have to research and choose one methodically? Well, there are a lot of reasons. These turtles live several decades and some can clear a century. The environmental conditions are important to think about before buying a turtle. If you buy a turtle that is ill suited to your area, it may die, which you wouldn't want. A turtle should be bought matching the environmental conditions of the place you are currently living in. Your first turtle should be a hardy species, not one with a reputation for being problematic. Now, we'll flip through the introduction of some of the species before talking about their living conditions and nutrition requirements.

Chapter 1. Questions to Answer Before You Buy

Turtles and tortoises can be intriguing, enjoyable pets, but they are not ideal for everyone. A great many pet chelonians die because their humans did not get what they expected when they brought one home. Here are some things you need to think about and weigh up so you can decide if a turtle or tortoise is really the right choice of pet for you.

Are you looking for affection?

Turtles and tortoises are not like dogs and cats. While they may learn to appreciate you as the creature that feeds and cares for them, turtles are not affectionate creatures. They may like you in their own way, but they're not going to show it the way other four-legged companions do. In addition, chelonians are not terribly fond of being held or carried. Turtles and tortoises will frequently urinate—or worse—when picked up, and being carried around will stress them out. Some of these animals are perpetually grumpy and will bite your finger if you get too close, no matter how long you've had them. Others may pull their limbs into their shells and hide if you try to touch them.

Now, not all turtles and tortoises are like this. One breeder of Yellow Belly Sliders has one that actually enjoys being petted on top of his head and will beg for attention as much as he begs for food. But generally speaking, you're going to be watching this pet much more than playing with it. If you're looking for an outpouring of love, this is probably not the right pet for you.

Are you looking for a lifetime companion?

Turtles and tortoises are not like hamsters. While a lot of them die after a couple of years, those deaths are usually caused by poor care, accidents, etc. When properly cared for, a turtle or tortoise you buy today will outlive you. These animals commonly live anywhere from 40 to more than 100 years. Many don't even reach maturity for 10-15 years or more. If you aren't ready for this kind of commitment, one that may lead to your grandchildren one day inheriting your chelonian, this is probably not the right pet for you.

Are you willing to spend time and energy on a pet every day?
Turtles and tortoises are not like fish. You cannot just toss a few flakes of food in the water in the morning and forget about them for the rest of the day. Terry Kilgore, a breeder of Red-footed Tortoises and Spotted Turtles, warns that too many would-be chelonian owners don't realize how much work is involved in caring for these animals. "Be ready to spend at least an hour—if not more—every day, maintaining and taking care of them," he said. If you travel a lot, if your schedule is extremely busy, or if you cannot otherwise commit to good daily care, this is probably not the right pet for you.

At this point, you may have decided you've read far enough, because clearly a turtle or tortoise will not fit into your lifestyle. Please don't feel bad. There is a perfect pet for you, but if you've realized a chelonian is not the one, it's much better to figure that out now rather than after you've bought one. If you're still interested in bringing a turtle or tortoise into your life, if you've decided that you're willing to commit to a lifetime pet who needs a lot from you without necessarily giving anything back, that's wonderful, but now is not the time to rush to the pet store or find a breeder. There are a few more things you need to be aware of before you purchase a chelonian.

How much is this going to cost?
Very common chelonians may cost you $5 to $15 (£4 to £12). In fact, some stores or dealers give turtles such as Red Eared Sliders away for free with the purchase of a tank and accessories. Beware of such offers. Usually these turtles are hatchlings that are illegal to sell because of their size (more on this shortly). The tank setup the store offers with the free or cheap turtle is almost always insufficient for the animal's needs. The Eastern Painted Turtle is a popular pet that

costs roughly $15 or £12; it grows from 5 to 10 inches in length and lives up to 25 years. Red Eared Sliders can live up to 70 years and may cost anywhere from $7-$18 (£5-£15). A small Turtle is a dry land species that will grow up to 6 inches long and may cost $30 or £22; they live up to 40 years, although some turtles can reach 100 years old. Russian Tortoises are more expensive at $75 or £62. Sulcata Tortoises cost from $50 or £40 and can grow up to 2.5 feet long. Animals from reputable breeders, as well as uncommon species of turtles, can cost anywhere from $50/£40 to $1,200/£900 or more. There are a surprising number of collectors out there who will pay astronomical amounts for rare chelonians to add to their private zoo. But no matter how much or how little you pay for a chelonian, your biggest expenses will include providing a proper habitat, and veterinary care if the animal gets sick.

Of course you plan to care for your pet so well that it will always be healthy. The problem is that turtles, especially those caught in the wild, are shipped around the world and to pet stores in horrendous conditions. Most are already stressed and either highly susceptible to disease or already sick by the time they are put on display for you to buy. In the chapter on Health, we'll talk about how to look for a healthy pet before you buy. Even if yours does appear to be in good condition, you should take your new pet to a reptile-savvy veterinarian for a checkup, just to be sure. You'll find some links to help you find a good local vet in the Resources section of this book.

Setting up a proper aquatic habitat can start at $700 or £570, depending on what your chelonian needs; a dry terrarium may start as low as £150 or $200 for basic equipment. Whether feeding fresh food or commercially prepared pellets, you may spend $20-£16 per month on diet alone. Turtles and tortoises are not inexpensive pets.

Where can I find a turtle to buy?
Most pet stores, including the big chains such as PetsMart and Petco, will carry the most common turtle, the Red Eared Slider. Smaller boutique stores may also offer other species, though they

may not have any to offer, depending on local laws. If you know what species of turtle you want, you can look for a breeder, either located near you or via the Internet. Check with local reptile (herpetological, or herp) hobby and enthusiast clubs to find good breeders. You can also find out about herp shows coming to your area through these clubs. There is usually a good variety of turtle and tortoise species for sale at these shows and expos.

What kind of chelonian should I get?
With so many species to choose from, deciding what turtle is right for you can be difficult. You can find information on dozens of chelonians, including size, habitat and feeding requirements, later in this book. That information will help you pick out just the right animal, but here are the most basic questions to ask yourself to narrow down the choices a bit:
1) Do you want an indoor or outdoor pet?
2) How much room do you have? Many species grow surprisingly large, and even small turtles cover a lot of ground in their slow-moving way.

Are turtles legal where I live?
This is a very important consideration when thinking about adding a chelonian to your household, and one that doesn't have a very good answer: It depends. One law that most countries observe is a ban on selling turtles that are less than 4" (or 10cm) long. This is the shell length, not the entire length of the animal from nose to tail tip. The ban was enacted in the 1970s, after it became popular to sell tiny Red Eared Slider hatchlings as pets. Cases of salmonella poisoning skyrocketed, especially among children. Turtles and tortoises are frequent carriers of salmonella bacteria, which cause food poisoning symptoms such as horrible intestinal distress, vomiting, cramping, and which can be fatal to children or those whose immune system is compromised. Chelonians under 4" are easy for children to stick in their mouths, so sales were banned. This does not mean turtles and tortoises over 4" won't give you salmonella. Kids are just less likely

to put the whole turtle in their mouths. However, after handling any chelonian, or after cleaning its habitat, wash your hands (and anywhere the habitat water spills) thoroughly with soap and hot water. Your stomach will thank you.

There are still pet stores and dealers who sell turtles and tortoises smaller than 4". They are just doing so illegally. If they are caught, they will pay a fine and be required to dispose of all their illegal animals. However, there is a bit of a loophole in the law that says animals under 4" cannot be sold as pets, but can be sold for educational, scientific, export, or exhibit purposes. Many dealers will sell hatchlings as long as you agree that you're using the animal for education or scientific purposes—said with a wink, of course, because you both know you're buying a pet. In most places, buying or possessing a chelonian of less than 4" is NOT illegal, just selling them is against the law. However, in some states, the law is tighter, and buying a tiny chelonian will land you in trouble if you are found out. The federal version of this law does not apply to hobby breeders, those who are not running an actual commercial turtle farm or pet store, so you can safely acquire a hatchling from many breeders or local herp club members.

There are other laws to be aware of, and those are laws regarding certain chelonian species, particular to your city or state. For example, in Iowa, it is illegal to possess any turtle or tortoise species native to Iowa, but you may keep pets of non-native species. Georgia has a lengthy list of prohibited turtles, and snapping turtles are illegal to keep in many states. In several states and countries, you must have a license or permit and other official paperwork to keep certain species. You will need to contact your state or province's division of wildlife and ask what the laws are regarding keeping pet turtles and tortoises. While it is against the law to keep many species of wild-caught turtle or tortoise, you may be able to find a breeder and buy a captive-born animal. Again, you'll need to check your local laws to be sure. Some laws apply only to wild-caught, others apply to the species as a whole.

If you buy from a breeder, a reputable one will have breeding records to prove your animal isn't wild-caught. There are many species you might see in a pet store that are wild-caught, especially if the animal is over the 4" requirement. In fact, reptile expert Melissa Kaplan notes that turtles available at pet stores frequently have holes in their shells caused by the tools used to capture them. If the store cannot show evidence that they came from a breeder, Kaplan says you can be sure the turtles were wild-caught. Entire habitats in the wild now stand empty because every turtle or tortoise in the area was captured to be sold in the pet trade. If you're concerned about not giving profits to those people catching, and sometimes poaching, chelonians in the wild, make sure to ask the store where the animal came from.

Are turtles good pets for kids?
Turtles are not the ideal pets for a child, and there are many reasons why. First is the salmonella issue. Children are not the greatest hand washers in the world. With younger children, especially, you would need to supervise every physical contact between child and animal, enforcing good hygiene afterwards.

Children can be deadly to chelonians. It's difficult for a child to have a pet they cannot pick up, hold, squeeze, and love. Grabbing a pet turtle or tortoise to hug it can easily result in the animal being stressed, the animal biting or scratching the child, and the animal being dropped or thrown. Constant supervision is necessary when allowing a child access to a chelonian. In addition, there is too much daily maintenance to expect a child to care for the turtle or tortoise properly by themselves. With a cat, the child can feed it once a day and clean the litter a couple of times a week and the cat will be content.

Chelonians require attention every day, and water-loving species need serious, frequent habitat cleaning. Children can certainly help accomplish the chores associated with a turtle, but they cannot be entirely responsible for it, nor can they be expected to do it alone unless they are older teenagers. So, are you still interested in getting a turtle or tortoise? Or do you already have one, and you're just trying to get to the parts of the book that will teach you how to properly care for your pet? Let's forge ahead and look at habitats for both turtles.

Chapter 2. Starting with the Right Turtle

Turtles can be fascinating, beautiful, fun pets. An important key in owning a turtle is to start out with one that is healthy. Unfortunately, not all places sell healthy or even legal turtles. You should always purchase your turtle from a trustworthy place and stay away from what I call "Turtle Mills" which are places that don't care about the well-being of these creatures. They only care about selling them to make money. A good quality breeder or store will give you some sort of a health guarantee in writing. Even if it is only for 24 hours, this will give you enough time to take it to a qualified Reptile Veterinarian for their approval. Now let's look at the 6 Common Turtles species to choose from.

The 6 Common Turtle Species
These 6 subspecies are:
1) Easter Turtle
2) Three-toed Turtle
3) Gulf Coast Turtle
4) Florida Turtle
5) Mexican Turtle
6) Yucatan Turtle

These 6 subspecies differ only slightly in their outside appearance, mainly in their color and the patterns on their Carapace. Yet all Common Turtles have a small to medium size head with a very distinctive upper jaw that is hooked up. Most adult males have red irises and most adult females have yellowish brown irises. When a male is an adult they will have stockier, shorter, curved claws on their hind feet. Their tails will be thicker and longer than females.

The Common Turtles name has derived from how its shell is structured. The upper shell, which is called the Carapace, is a high, domed shell that is connected to the lower shell called the Plastron. These two parts of the shell, the Carapace and Plastron, are connected. This system allows for the turtle to go inside its shell and close it, thus being able to seal its vulnerable head and limbs from predators while being inside its impregnable box. The Carapace is brown in color and usually has a variable pattern of colors like orange or yellow spots, lines, blotches or bars. The Plastron is a darker brown and is usually uniformly colored. Sometimes it will have even darker smudges or blotches.

Eastern Turtle

The Carapace has mainly a darker brown to almost a black look and it is not uncommon for it to be streaked with yellow. Its Carapace can have orange and red blotches on it as well. The plastron runs between yellow and black. It can have patterns but sometimes it will have no patterns. The Eastern Turtle's skin is dark with red to yellow blotches, while some males will have reddish sunburn looks on their skin. These color patterns make a perfect camouflage in their habitat, which is usually the forest floor. Most of these turtles will have 4 toes on their hind feet but at times you will see one that only has 3. The Eastern Turtle usually is found in woodland settings. Quite often during "cooling" or hibernation, they can be found in pastures and marshy meadows. They will establish a territory that is usually between 2 to 11 acres. Somewhere in their territory there will be a body of water such as a pond or creek. When fully grown, they will range between 4 ½" to 6" long. The world record was a whopping 7.8" long.

Three-toed Turtle

The Three-toed Turtle's habitat ranges from Missouri down to Texas and across to Georgia in the United States. These areas are ideal temperature wise and for their humid grasslands, woodlands, marshes and thickets. Their Carapace is commonly a uniformed olive in color and their Plastron is a lighter shade of olive. However, like the Eastern Turtle, there are variations in color; some Carapaces can be a darker, almost brown looking olive and some Plastrons can have blotchy black markings. Mostly they will have very few yellow markings. Their head, neck and arms have red, yellow and orange blotches. Males are predominately more colorful than females, but I have seen several females that have brilliant color markings. Their Carapace is typically more domed, with the highest point being at the back of its shell. Sometimes they will have 3 toes on their hind feet but mostly they will have 4. They mature in length typically between 4" to 5", while some can grow up to 6".

Gulf Coast Turtle
The Gulf Coast Turtle is larger than the other turtles. The Carapace is a keeled shaped and is elongated with the marginal scutes being flared. Its Carapace is also a darker brown and can be almost black. The Plastron is even darker with a deep brown to jet-black coloring. Males can quite often have white patches on their head and in some cases the head may be almost all white.

Florida Turtle
Their Carapace is elongated and slightly narrow. It will usually have streaks of thin light yellowish lines running lengthways. The Plastron is often a brownish-yellow and sometimes will have brown streaks. The head and neck are a dark brown with yellow streaks. A big distinction between the other species is that the Florida Turtle will have brown eyes, while the other male subspecies will have red eyes.

Mexican Turtle
The Mexican Turtle is rarely sold as a pet. I have only seen a handful in all my years of caring for these turtles. When fully grown, it has a longer, domed Carapace with a hump on the 3rd vertebral scute, thus making this turtle unique. The Carapace color is a medium brown and it has a darker brown coloring on the sutures, giving the appearance of an outline around its Carapace. Its head and neck are grey or brown and it will sometimes have light spotting on the sides of its head.

Yucatan Turtle

The Yucatan Turtle is listed under "endemic species"; this means that the entire known species is located in a single area, which is on the Yucatan Peninsula of Mexico. Thus, because this subspecies is located so far away from the other subspecies, it is heavily isolated from any of the other subspecies. Years after it was discovered, it was believed not to be a subspecies of the Common Turtle, but over time it was discovered that it was. You might have guessed by now that acquiring one of these in different parts of the world is almost impossible. There are only a few Yucatan Turtles being kept in captivity in the United States. This turtle can reach to around 6" in length. The male Yucatan Turtle is unique regarding its pigmentation. For example, some will have a white face that is so strong that it can look like it is wearing makeup.

Male or Female, which is best?

For their day to day behavior both sexes act basically the same, so it does not really matter which sex you decide to purchase, unless you want to breed. Both sexes make excellent pets.It is extremely difficult to tell the difference between the male and female until they are fully grown, and even then it can be hard. Until the turtle's Carapace length reaches 3 to 3 ½ inches long (7.6 to 8.9 cm), it is extremely hard to tell which sex they are. If you want a certain sex you should purchase your turtle from an experienced handler. They can tell you which sex it is and they will put it in writing.

You can tell a male from a female by looking for these differences:

1) Most American male species have bright red, ruby-reddish or pink eyes, whereas females have brown eyes.
2) Adult males will have greenish or faded yellowish heads, whereas mature females have dark brown heads.
3) A male's plastrons are concaved; this helps during mating.
4) Male hind legs are strong and thick with large claws, females have thinner legs and their claws are finer.

14

5) Male tales are thick and longer than the females.

6) The male's vent area (opening of the cloacae) is located well beyond the edge of its shell; the female's vent area is located closer to her body. The vent areas for both sexes help them to place their cloacae next to each other easily during copulation (sexual intercourse).

Adult female turtles tend to do well with other female turtles, and they tend to get along well with other 'mild temperament' breeds of turtles.

Male Turtles do not get along with other male turtles, especially during mating season. If males do not coexist properly with each other, then you need to provide separate housing for each of them. A male can usually be with a female turtle all year round, but when mating season starts, males can become quite aggressive towards females. They can be extremely persistent in trying to breed with the female. Females can easily become stressed and sometimes can be injured.

How to Determine its Age

For a female or male turtle to become a fully-grown adult it takes about 10 years. Turtles have been known to live up to a 100 years, but this is highly unusual as most live to around the ages of 35 to 40. A turtle will grow about one-third of the its fully-grown size at approximately 3 years. In the next 3 years the turtle will have reached about two-thirds of its full size. Keep in mind that this is only a rough rule of thumb, as a turtle's growth depends on the environment that it lives in. How much food and water is available or how long the season of plentiful food is play a role.

The growth rate of a turtle slows down as it ages, but as I said, when it reaches the age of 10 it should be fully-grown or close to it. Some people believe that you can count the rings that grow around the turtle's shell to determine its age, but this is not true; these rings only tell the turtle's growth rate. Young turtles may grow several rings around its shell in just one year. Wild turtles usually stop growing rings around the age of 20. I have found that captive turtles that have consistent eating patterns can sometimes go for one full year without growing any rings.

Best & Worst Places to Purchase Your Turtle
I don't feel comfortable purchasing a turtle that I personally can't go see in its living environment. Think about it, the advantage in purchasing one of these turtles from a reputable pet store or breeder is that you can actually go inside and see for yourself what living conditions your potential turtle is living in. You can see if they are healthy, well cared for and enjoying themselves, and that they are not stressed from dirty, overcrowding, and/or neglected conditions. Imagine a turtle that is flown and delivered to your mailbox. It has been handled by lots of different people during the trip. Do you think it will be stressed out when it gets to you? I think so. The fact is, even if you purchase a stressed-out turtle and you provide it with the perfect care, it could have been so stressed that it will become ill and die in a short amount of time.

Even though companies that sell turtles on the Internet have a guarantee, often turtles will live just past the guaranteed expiration date, and then die. The turtle must also be kept in the correct temperatures during any transport. If you decide that you want to purchase a turtle that will be shipped in the mail, just make sure they make every effort to provide a safe and comfortable situation for your turtle. You do not have to worry about buying one of these turtles from a reputable pet shop. Quite often you can find excellent breeders locally, this way you can go visit to see how the turtles are cared for. You can ask the breeder if you can see the turtle's breeding parents to see how healthy their lives have been. The point is, years ago buying a turtle was risky, but with the current regulations it is much, much safer.

Checklist for Choosing a Healthy Turtle
When purchasing your pet turtle, you want to make sure you are starting out with one that is healthy and has been well cared for.

1. Check to See How Clean Its Environment Is
Again, this is the advantage of being able to actually go in and see the environment your potential turtle has been raised in. Dirty water, unsanitary conditions, and overcrowding can easily cause a turtle to be stressed and susceptible to diseases.

2. What Is Its Demeanor?
Pick up the turtle. A healthy one will probably make defensive motions by pulling its legs into its shell and/or trying to get away from you. It should also be alert, full of life, and be responsive. Remember, turtles are reptiles and temperature variations will cause a turtle to move in a lethargic way, especially if it is cold.

3. Check Out The Condition of its Body
These turtles should not be fat and have rolls of skin on their necks or legs, nor should they be emaciated. Their bodies should be full, supple and healthy with the skin being able to move back quickly when you gently pull it. When you pick it up, it should be solid and heavy for its size. Its shell should be hard (soft shells could be a sigh of MBD, Metabolic Bone Disease), smooth, with no lumps and not flaky. There should also be no unhealed cracks in the Carapace. Both the skin and the shell should have no scrapes, cuts, cracks or defects on them, as any one of these could become infected at anytime.

The Plastron should have no cuts or cracks and the hinge should also have no damage. Shell rot can often occur on the Plastron, so you should look for any peeling scutes or a bad smelling odor.
Cracked or dry skin can be a sign that the turtle was kept in very dry conditions.

4. Check out the Tail Area
See if it has or had diarrhea and check for any indications of parasites, infections or swelling around the anus.

5. Check Its Eyes
This is an excellent way to see if this turtle is healthy. If its eyes are not clear, clean, wide open, or if you see any seeping or crusty material on them, then something is wrong. Continually closed or swollen eyes are definite signs that a turtle has an illness or infection.

6. Check Its Mouth
The saliva should not be thick or stringy. When looking inside its mouth, all of the skin should be pink in color, with no foamy bubbles or coatings and it should also be smooth. If you see a grayish or pale pink color or little green, yellow or white spots on the inside of its mouth or on its tongue, these are signs of mouth rot or some other type of illness.

7. Check Its Face and Head
If you see any swelling or that both sides of the head are not proportionate, this could be a sign of abscesses, Metabolic Bone Disease or other infections.

8. Look for Any Respiratory Diseases
How do its nostrils look? Are they clean and clear of any discharge? If you see any mucous, this can be a sign of a respiratory illness. Other signs that the turtle is sick are if it breathes through its mouth or makes a wheezing, clicking or bubbling sound when it breathes. A respiratory infection can also cause a turtle to walk and swim lopsided.

9. Check How It Moves
A healthy turtle should move and swim with grace and strength. Any weakness can be a sign of Metabolic Bone Disease or other illnesses.

Chapter 3. Setting Up The Environment

Outside Or Inside?

I prefer keeping my Painted Turtles inside. This way, I have total control over their environment, such as temperatures, water quality, cleanliness, keeping it safe from predators, etc. Having turtles in my home lets me be more interactive with them, too. Turtles that see you often become familiar with you and therefore are more comfortable when you approach them, not to mention they provide lots of watching entertainment. Some climates are so harsh that it is too difficult to keep a turtle outside, but you might live in a climate that is more conducive for keeping your turtle outdoors. Whether you decide to keep your turtle inside or outside, this book will show you how to create the right set-up.

Where to Purchase Supplies

I am not one to recommend a brick and mortar retail store or an online retail store because I don't want to seem biased. When purchasing your supplies, you should buy quality products, check for the best pricing and, whoever you do business with, make sure they provide a money back guarantee. Most reptile stores don't employ sales people that have knowledge about turtles. Use my experience written in this book and don't let an unqualified salesperson talk you into purchasing the wrong products. In the costs section later in this chapter is a list of products that you will need to purchase to have a high quality set-up for your turtle. Each product has by it the price that it should cost. The price that is shown is what I pay at my local retail reptile store, and at online retail reptile stores. This price sheet is an excellent guideline that will help keep you from paying too much.

Your turtle will need a container that will hold the right amount of water, give it the right amount of space to thrive in, and, all of the products needed to keep its environment functioning correctly. It is important that you set it up so that it is easily maintained. The less time you spend with maintenance means the more time you can enjoy your turtle. I prefer to keep my turtle in either an all-glass or Plexiglas aquarium. This way I can watch them in their environment. The downside to purchasing one of these aquariums is that they do cost a bit more. If you would rather use plastic containers such as a plastic swimming pool, large plastic storage box, or plastic tubs, these too will work well. Whichever one you decide on, just make sure it is clean and water tight.

What to Purchase/ Building Your Turtle's Home
The Basic Container
This habitat set-up is by far the most popular. It is reasonably priced, sets up quickly and is easy to maintain. All you need is some type of container that will hold water and be high enough for your turtle's size (Painted Turtles have been known to escape over sides that are too low).
You'll need to have the following equipment to go along with the container:

1) Screen top to stop your turtle from getting out (like I said, they can be expert escape artists).
2) Temperature thermometer with a humidity gauge.
3) Underwater heater with guard so your turtle can't break it.
4) Bottom filters work great for 10 gallons or less of water. For larger containers, I strongly recommend a Canister Filtration System.
5) Two lights with fixtures: 1 x UVA/UVB Reptile Light and 1 x basking red light. You can save money and just put your lights on the screen top.
6) Gravel for the bottom of the container (not necessary but certain species love to rummage through the rocks).

The Ultimate Container

This habitat set-up is the best, but it does take more work and money to set it up, as it is a bigger playground for your turtle). The layout of this container should be 30% surface for walking and bask on with hiding areas and the other 70% is for swimming. The depth of the water should be 2 X the length of your turtle's bottom shell. Example: A 4" long shell (measure the length of the Plastron x 2 = the water depth of 8 inches (deeper is even better as they love to swim).

You need to put a walking surface area inside the container. You can purchase a display that has this walking surface built in it and simply place it securely inside the container. This is the simplest way to install a walking surface. Just go to your local pet store and buy a kit that has everything already in it. The kits can even come with waterfalls and a small stream. I have done this but I also like to build my own, and it's not that difficult. Where the water joins the walking surface, put a stick or something that will serve as a ladder so your turtle will be able to climb out of the water and onto the walking surface. You can build your own walking surface out of Plexiglas. This can be accomplished by using a piece of precisely cut Plexiglas. Measure the length and width you want your Plexiglas to be cut and then go to a hardware store. You can purchase the Plexiglas and have it cut to your dimensions. Use silicone sealer to seal in the Plexiglas the sides and let it dry for 24 hours. You can also put corkboard on top of the Plexiglas, which will provide better footing for your pet turtle.

I had a turtle that never did understand the concept of an all-glass aquarium. It constantly kept hitting the sides of the aquarium, so much so that I thought it would hurt itself. I solved this problem by putting a colored cloth material on the outside of the aquarium walls at the water's highest level. The turtle finally figured out that a wall was there and stopped hitting it. Once he learned that, I removed the cloth from the sides of the aquarium. If you have a container/tub without a lid, you need to make one, as this will keep your turtle from escaping and for outside set-ups it will keep predators out.

Hardware cloth is an excellent material to make your cover out of. It is made out of metal and has big enough wire woven squares so you can see your turtle but it can't get out. You can also set your lights on top of it. You can get by not using a lid cover if the container design is such that the turtle can't escape (see picture below). This set-up works because the walls are steep and they have no grip for the turtle to be able to climb out of it. In addition, the water and basking area is low enough that the turtle's only choice is to enjoy its beautiful set up. I strongly recommend, if your turtle is outside, to put some type of cover over it like hardware cloth, as it is excellent in keeping predators out.

Outdoor Habitat
Some climates are more desirable for setting up an outdoor environment. When you build an outdoor habitat you can be really creative in your designs, usually because of all of the space. But there are several things that you must have in the habitat in order for it to be successful. Listed below is the important equipment you will need to make it an excellent living environment for your pet turtle. You can use a plastic container, a small paddling pool or even one made out of cement as long as it does not leak. You can also purchase pond plastic containers at most hardware stores. You will need:

1) Filtration System
2) Basking Area
3) Gravel and Rocks
4) Shade Area
5) Protective Fencing
6) Heater (some areas are too hot and don't require a heater to keep the water at the right temperature)
The bigger the container, the easier it is to maintain.

a) Container: You can either put your container in or above the ground. I prefer one that is in the ground with a walking area around the edge. When you install the pool, make one end a little higher and have some type of drainage for excess water to run out and go away from the pool. This will be an effective way to stop an overflow from a rain downpour.

b) Filtration System: There are several brands that you can purchase from any pet store. My favorite is a simple submersible pump that has a return design that sets on the bottom of the pool. Simply connect a hose to it and run the hose to some place in the pool. The filter will filter the water and send the clean water through the hose, which will lead back into the pool. You can hang the hose high enough to cause a waterfall effect. This will cause the water to have movement; turtles that enjoy the water movement will congregate towards this area.

c) Basking Area: You can put in a small stump, chunk of wood, thick log or a rock that has flat surface. This set-up needs to have a way that your turtle can easily climb out of the water and onto it. Your turtle will get plenty of UVA/UVB from the sun.

d) Gravel and Rocks: Put small, clean gravel on the bottom of the floor along with enough rocks so that your turtle can explore around them. Light colored rocks make it easier to see your turtle when it is on the bottom. In addition, put some leaves in the pool; your turtle will use them to hide under. You can use cattails and reeds for vegetation, as your turtle will not eat these.

e) Shade Area: Build a shady area so your turtle can hide and/or cool down. You can simply put some wood in such a way that there is a place for your turtle to go and hide in it. You can also put artificial plants and large rocks and set them up for a shady area. Another way is to use all three to build one. Be creative here, your turtle will love to hide under all of these things and they also provide shade.

f) Protective Fencing: You want the fence to be secure enough to keep predators out and your turtle in. You can buy pre-made fencing from most hardware stores that are secure and will keep predators out. If you are handy, you can build it yourself and save money – the important point is, make it predator proof!

g) Heater: The water has to be kept at the right temperature (see section on setting temperatures in this chapter). Therefore, you will need to purchase an outdoor water heater if you live in areas where the sun's heat can't maintain your desired temperature. However, if you live in a place that provides enough heat, you don't need to buy a heater. For areas that are perfect in the summers but so cold in the winters that you can't keep the water warm enough, you can keep your turtle outside in the summer and inside during the winter.

h) Thermometers: Make sure you purchase water thermometers that are easy to read. I put one at each end of the pool just in case one fails.

Indoor Environments
The Filter
Turtles eat and defecate in their water, so it can become dirty fast. You don't want to be changing the water all the time. The solution is a high quality water filter and the best types are Canister Filters for containers that hold more than 10 gallons. I've found them to be the most effective at keeping my turtle's tank cleaner and for longer.

My canister filtration system can work 3 times better than the other types of filters I have used. They do cost more, but they will do a better job cleaning and therefore will save you a lot of maintenance time. They are also easy to clean. Don't be tight on spending money here, as the best filtration system is well worth the extra cost. If you have a 10-gallon or smaller tank, there are several types of fairly inexpensive water filters that use a pump to filter the water. You can find these at any store that carries aquarium supplies.

I recommend purchasing one of these, as a canister filtration system would be way over kill, and why spend the extra money when you don't need it. It is a general "rule" that for turtles, you should have double the filtration required than for fish, as turtles are a lot messier. If your container holds 20 gallons of water, then get a filter that is designed for a 40-gallon aquarium, as it will make maintaining a lot easier.

The Basking Area

Basking areas solve your turtle's need to warm up and dry out completely. You can make a basking area on the land's surface or have a platform just sticking out of the water. I like both ways. It just depends how you want your turtle's environment set up, so it's up to you. The important thing about basking areas is they must be low enough to the water so your turtle can easily climb onto it and still be raised up above the water's surface. If your platform is slippery or unstable, your turtle might not want to use it, so make sure it is solid, secure and provides some type of gripping to help your turtle climb up.

You can make platforms out of rocks. They have to be fairly flat on top for your turtle to climb and rest on. Use darker colored rocks, as they will absorb the basking light's heat, which turtles love. Before I put any rocks (or anything) into the water, I thoroughly wash it. Rock platforms are natural, solid, and free.

The Basking Light

Use a red heat lamp that is made for reptiles. I use incandescent light bulbs with ceramic light bulb sockets (these sockets are safer around water). They are efficient to operate, last longer and provide the right heat for the basking areas. The higher the bulb's wattage, the more heat it emits. The size that you want will correspond with the size of your container. The bulb's package will tell you how much of an area the bulb can heat (see setting temperatures in this section). You can place your light fixture on the top of your container or the basking light fixture can be purchased with a stand. You will also need to cool down your turtle's home at night by 8 to 10 degrees. This will create and mimic the turtle's natural habitat of day/night. You can do this by turning off the UVA/UVB Reptile

Light (this light should be on 12 to 14 hours per day) and just leave on the red basking light. Or you can leave the red basking light on, turn off the Reptile Light, and turn on a red nighttime light. The bulb needs to be red in color because turtles have a hard time seeing the color red. The nightlight will keep the habitat from getting too cold. Install these lights high enough above the water's surface so that your turtle cannot touch them or get a "sun burn", as these bulbs do get hot.

UVA/UVB Reptile Lighting

Your turtle needs to have UVA and UVB rays to stay healthy, and these bulbs also provide vitamin D3, which your turtle needs to metabolize calcium and phosphorus for good health. If your turtle can be outside in the sun for a few hours each week then it will receive enough of these rays. But if your turtle is going to be kept indoors all of the time, you will need to purchase a full-spectrum light bulb or fluorescent light (this bulb supplies both of these rays) for your turtle to be able to stay healthy. The light will have stamped on it UVA AND UVB REPTILE. My favorite reptile day light is by Energy Savers Unlimited. It is a full-spectrum fluorescent light design for turtles, and comes in lengths of 18-48 inches. Full-spectrum lights loose their effectiveness with time. In your caretaking charts, record when you purchased the light and then replace it in 6 months. The best place to mount this light is usually in the center of your container for an overall lighting effect. When you purchase this light from your reptile store, you can also purchase a fixture for it that will work for your specific container/aquarium. You will want to have the light about 6-15 inches above the top of your turtle's shell.

You are dealing with electricity, so make sure that you install the electrical products correctly. All electrical cords should be connected to a ground-fault interrupter, which shuts off the current if anything happens. This makes it so you and your turtle cannot receive an electric shock. You can purchase one at a hardware store. Hardware stores sell timers for these lights so that you can set them to go on/off when you want them to. Remember, it is best to follow the seasons' daytime/nighttime hours to give the best "natural effect" for your turtle. If you don't want to do this, a good rule of thumb is to have 12 to 14 hours of daylight and 10 to 12 hours of nighttime. For all of your lights, make sure they do not shine through anything such as glass; this will reduce the basking lights' heat and the all important rays provided by the full-spectrum lighting.

The Heaters
If you have a very large container and it needs more heat than what the basking and UVA/UVB lights can emit, you can heat the rest of the container's area by using an incandescent light bulb with the correct fixture set up. This should be installed on the opposite side of the basking light with the UVA/UVB light in the middle. This incandescent light bulb needs to emit less heat than the basking light (see setting temperatures in this section).

Your turtle needs different temperatures in its environment. This way it can go to different areas so it can either cool down or warm up; your turtle will know how warm it wants and needs to be. All lights should be installed high enough so that your turtle can't touch them or get sun burnt. In addition, have heat ventilation holes above the lights so heat can't build up above the fixture. For smaller containers, you do not want this light as the basking light, as the UVA/UVB Reptile Light and the water's temperature will provide enough heat for your turtle's environment.

The water needs to be heated with an underwater heater or submersible heater. These heaters come with a built-in thermostat. The heat output for your heater that you'll need depends upon how much water you want to heat up. The information on the heaters will tell you how much volume it will heat up. Follow the directions that show you how to install the heater. Depending on how much water you are heating, it usually takes about 48 hours to heat it up to the right temperature.

Thermometers
Because you are going to heat your turtle's habitat higher in the day compared to at night, a helpful thermometer is one that records the highest/lowest temperatures in a 24-hour period. This will tell you if you need to adjust the temperatures. You can also purchase a regular thermometer. You can read them in the daytime and at night (they just require a little more work on your part).

For bigger habitat set-ups where the temperature is colder on the opposite end away from the basking area, you should install a thermometer on the cooler side and put one on the basking side. Place all thermometers in a setting that you can easily read. I use water thermometers because thermostat water heaters with built in thermometers have been known to fail and I like to be on the safe side. With these 3 thermometers, you will be able to regulate your turtle's home accurately.

Hygrometer Humidity Gauge
This gauge will tell you what the humidity level is. You can purchase a thermometer that also has a humidity gauge with it. I like to keep the humidity at 90%.

Keeping the water pure and clean for your turtle is vital. If you use water that has certain additives, it can kill your turtle. So water quality is crucial, but how can you find out the quality of your water before you put your turtle in it? You can call your local water supplier, which is either the water district or the city that you live in, and ask them what is in your water and if it is safe for your turtle. If your water is from a well, you can take a sample to one of these two local services and they will analyze it for you at no cost to you.

At your pet store you can purchase a kit that will test the water for chemicals, acidity, alkaline, hardness and chlorine. Most city water has chlorine in it. If the water needs to be treated to make it safe, your local pet store will have the right treatments for it.
The water/swimming area should also have installed a hose that allows air to be pumped into the water. This will create oxygen and movement in the water; a system like this can be bought at any pet store. Some filtration systems have this built in them.

Drinking Water
I use something as simple as a clean jar lid to put my turtle's drinking water in. It is low enough for your turtle to easily drink out of it and it is easy for you to pick up and clean. I put the lid on the walking surface. If you don't have a walking surface, don't worry, as your turtle will drink from its swimming water. This is another reason that you need to keep its swimming water clean.

Don't be fooled by thinking that rainwater is safe; you can easily have acid rain or other toxic chemicals in it.

Setting Up Its Home
One of the many decisions you'll make when deciding to get a chelonian as a pet is whether you want a land-based or water-based pet. This is a huge decision, not only because it narrows down your list of species to choose from, it also determines what sort of set-up you're going to have to buy or create.

We'll go into specific needs for each species later in the book, but for now, let's look at basic setups to give you an overview of what turtles and tortoises require. This is a good place to mention that almost all male turtles are smaller than the female of their species, which means buying a male will result in smaller habitat requirements.

If you're going to keep your turtle indoors, you'll need a large container. Glass and acrylic aquariums work fine, though large, Rubbermaid-type containers can work for some species. Stock tanks used to provide water for livestock work very well, though you can't see through the sides.

You may want to start with a smaller tank, especially if you're getting a hatchling or juvenile animal, but keep in mind that as the turtle grows you will have to buy bigger setups, including new lighting and filtration systems. It is often less expensive in the long run to buy the proper tank for the adult size of your turtle to begin with. For example, you may start with a 20-gallon aquarium for your female Red Belly Cooter, but end up needing a 125-gallon tank by the time she reaches adult size. Rather than graduating from 20 gallons to 55, then to 75, then to 125, stockpiling old aquariums as you go along, consider starting with 125 gallons.

One thing to consider is where you will place the tank. Some people want to keep the tank in the family room or kitchen where most of the family's time is spent in order to give the turtle lots of attention. Unfortunately, this causes unhealthy stress to many turtles. It's best to place your turtle's habitat in an area that is calmer.

Once you have the tank, you'll still have several things to buy. The setup of the tank depends a lot on what kind of turtle you have. Some, like Softshells, spend almost all their time in the water so they don't need a lot of dry land to walk around on. Others, such as Spotted Turtles, spend less time in the water and more basking and exploring, so they need more dry land in their enclosure. If you get into breeding, the female will need a dry area she can nest in, so the setup you start with may evolve later on. Let's look at what needs to go in the tank.

Substrate
This is the material that makes up the land portion of the habitat. While substrate is often used to cover the floor of the water portion

as well, many owners choose to leave the water part of the habitat bare. It doesn't look quite as nice as a layer of gravel on the bottom of the tank, but it is easier to clean and there's no chance that the turtle will try to swallow bits of gravel or rock. This approach won't work with some species. Softshells enjoy burying themselves in sand, so they really need an appropriate substrate.

Acceptable substrates vary with the turtle species, as noted in the species specifics section, but here are some of the options:
a) Sand: Many turtles are very fond of sand, but it wreaks havoc on filtration systems because the turtles stir it up so frequently. It is not an easy substrate for a keeper to live with.

b) Aquarium or Pea Gravel: Available in different sizes, this gravel is commonly used in turtle setups, though if you have a turtle that likes to swallow stones, it's best to use either a larger substrate the turtle can't eat, or the smallest diameter gravel which won't clog the turtle's intestines. Pea gravel is available at home improvement stores in larger quantities and lower prices than aquarium gravel.
c) River rock: These smooth rocks are usually big enough that turtles won't try to swallow them. Plus, their size creates interesting climbing opportunities for turtles and places for them to explore. However, make sure your turtle won't hit the rocks when diving into the water from the basking platform, or it may suffer shell cracks or other injury.

Water and water heaters
Tap water is usually fine for turtles, unless you have really bad water, or water that is heavily chlorinated. You can use bottled water, of course, though that will prove expensive with a large setup and regular water changes. If you have a commercial filter on your tap already, the water will be fine. If you're concerned about the water, you can use one of the animal-safe conditioners designed to neutralize the water, such as ReptiSafe. As far as water pH (acidity/alkalinity) goes, there are some species that have particular

requirements, but those turtles are not recommended for the novice owner.

Some turtles like their water in the low 70s, which is about room temperature in many households. Use a thermometer to test the water. If it stays in the correct range, you don't need a water heater. If it fluctuates too much or stays too cold, you'll need a heater. A submersible aquarium heater is fine, but a heater guard is a really good idea, both to keep the turtle from harming itself and to protect the heater from an active turtle.

Basking platform
All turtles need a place they can get out of the water on occasion and get completely dry, even underneath. In fact, some species spend a great deal of time sunning themselves out of the water. For that, you need a basking platform of some kind.
You can use commercially produced plastic platforms, or create your own. Some keepers choose a thick, flat piece of driftwood or pile up rocks with a flat rock on top. As long as it is secure and not going to fall over or slip when your turtle climbs aboard, and it's large enough to hold your turtle completely out of the water, that's what matters. The rest is just aesthetics and entirely up to you. One very creative way to provide a basking platform for a larger turtle is to build a separate box, complete with basking light, that fits on top of one end of the aquarium, above the water line.

Other furnishings
Turtles often need places to hide and things to investigate in their tanks. Plus, many turtles who like deep water also need things they can stand on underwater when they get tired, so they can stick their nose out of the water to breathe. Driftwood, fake log structures, and large rocks all make excellent habitat furnishings. When setting up the habitat, just make sure there are no large rocks that a turtle might hit when diving from the basking platform.

Plants

Many turtle species in the wild live in areas with abundant vegetation around the water, and some prefer water with a lot of plant life in it as well. Because turtles tend to disturb plant roots, many keepers choose plastic or silk plants to decorate habitats. Choose as many or as few as you wish.

Real aquatic plants can be used, if you prefer. It isn't easy to keep real plants alive, particularly those that may be uprooted when the turtle is active. Two plants, java fern and java weed, are easy to use because they are not planted in substrate. These plants can float free, or be tied to a structure, log, or other piece of habitat furniture. Anacharis is another good plant, but it will be chewed up by plant-loving turtles. Dealing with real plants can add to the headache of general habitat care and cleaning, but the plants do look good in the tank, if you're willing to do the work.

Tank cover

Turtles are not only great swimmers, they are strong climbers. If they are able to reach the top of the tank, they can get out, drop to the floor and either suffer injury from the drop or get into all sorts of trouble once on the ground. A cover over the tank will prevent this from happening. A cover also makes it easier to suspend lighting over the tank.

The best type of cover is a metal screen, especially if you attach it with clips to keep strong turtles from pushing it off. You can place the light bar for your turtles directly over the screen, cutting holes in the screen as necessary for the filtration system and water heater cord. Aquarium hoods with glass over the light won't work unless you remove the glass, because the glass will filter important UVB light.

Lighting

Lack of good lighting has harmed many turtles in captivity. A full-spectrum bulb is supposed to provide both UVA and UVB rays, like sunlight, but it doesn't do as thorough a job as turtles need. Real, unfiltered sunlight is always best, but letting the sun shine directly on your tank is a recipe for overheating disasters.

Here is a good way to provide enough correct light, the UVB your indoor turtle needs in order to stay healthy, and the right heat for the basking spot:
Use a bulb that offers full-spectrum light, such as ReptiSun 5.0 or the Iguana Light 5.0. Place this bulb in an aquarium hood, or in a fluorescent bulb fixture placed over a screen top. Use a UVB-producing basking lamp, which will also generate heat. PowerSun, Mega-Ray and UV-Heat are all very popular with experienced turtle keepers. These bulbs are a bit more expensive to buy than others, but they will produce UVB at least twice as long as other bulbs, so you won't need to replace them as often (regular fluorescent UVB bulbs wear out after about six months).

Many turtles will do fine in the dark when their enclosure cools to room temperature, unless you keep your room below 70 degrees. During the winter, in a cooler room, or for turtles requiring higher heat, you'll need a ceramic heat emitter at night, when the basking lamp is turned off.

Thermometers
It's essential to know what the temperatures are in your turtle's habitat. Generally, you'll want three thermometers, and tape thermometers work well. One should give you the temperature for the water, another should read the basking area, and another should be placed away from the basking area, so you can be sure there are cooler areas so your turtle can regulate its body temperature.

Filtration
This is an absolute necessity, unless you want to completely change the water in your tank every couple of days. Because turtles are so much dirtier than fish, you'll want to have a biological filtration

system that will keep the ammonia in the tank under control, as well as a mechanical component that filters waste, leftover food bits and such from the water. A good rule of thumb for filtration is to buy a system that is twice as strong as one recommended for an equal sized fish aquarium. For habitat cleaning, you'll also want a siphon, such as the Python system. This system can help you siphon water out of the tank and add fresh water back in. You'll also want a gravel vacuum. This will clean the bits and pieces out that get stuck in the substrate, at least in substrates smaller than river rock. To help keep the smell of the turtle's habitat under control, try adding charcoal to your water filter.

When setting up an indoor habitat, many people install a Plexiglass wall to divide their tank. On one side is the water, and the other is filled with substrate and becomes the land section. Be sure to place rocks, driftwood, or other furnishings to help your turtle climb out of the water and onto the land portion of the tank.

Turtles do best living in the outdoors, if you can manage it. For outdoor living, you'll need a stock tank or pond and a fence of some kind around the limits of the turtle's area. One recommendation is to create a pond or set the stock tank down in the ground, add appropriate plants both on the edge of the pond and in the water, add a pond filter and a water heater, if needed, then cover the entire area with an avian enclosure. The enclosure will keep your turtles where they are supposed to be, allow you a door for access, and prevent predators like dogs, cats, and raccoons from getting at the turtles. Don't forget to hang a basking light as well, though being outdoors will eliminate the need for a UVB bulb.

Good plants to use in this enclosure include floating plants, such as water lettuce or fairy moss, to help keep algae under control. Water hyacinths are great, but they are illegal to use in certain areas, such as Texas. Try Anacharis or tape grass if you want to plant the bottom of your pond, but with some turtles these plants may not survive long enough to be worth the expense. Watercress is also suitable. For good vegetation on your pond banks, try dwarf versions of cattails and rushes. Check with a nursery to see what grows best in your area and isn't poisonous to animals.

Some turtles, particularly those from tough temperate climates, can hibernate outside if the pond is at least two feet deep with a good, thick mud base for them to burrow into. Many specialists suggest bringing turtles indoors for the winter and not hibernating them. Check with your local herp society for recommendations specific to your area.

Except for the most aquatic ones, most species of turtle do walk around on land quite a bit, and if they are never allowed to, their muscles weaken. Even if your turtle lives indoors, give it a chance to walk around outside when weather permits.

Costs

The prices that I have listed below are for an indoor set up. Outdoor habitats usually cost less. These prices are what I usually pay, but, sometimes there are specials that you can take advantage of. You can buy a 55-gallon aquarium glass tank with a nice cabinet, filter, lid, lights, heater, thermometers and water treatment at a National Pet Store Chain for $350 or £280. This is an excellent price, but keep in mind it always pays to shop around, not just for price but also for quality. I am pricing everything out for a 20-gallon aquarium set-up. If you want a bigger set-up for your turtle, just remember that you will need bigger lights, heater and filters etc., which will cost more. The purpose of this section is to give you an idea of what you should be paying, as I believe this will keep you from paying too much.

The Set up Costs

Aquarium

A 20-gallon glass aquarium can cost $80 or £64.

Tub/Container

A 20-gallon plastic tub can cost about $8.00 or £6.40.

Canister Filter

A high quality 40-gallon canister filter can cost up to $196 or £158. I always use a bigger filter than what is required for my aquarium. It will keep the water cleaner much longer, which is great for you and your turtle.

Other Filters

You can purchase other types of filters that fit a 20-gallon tank and they will do a good job (you might have to clean it a little more often). The price drops drastically, as they range from $18.00 or £14.

Basking Light and Fixture

The right wattage light here can cost $5.50 or £4.20.

Full-Spectrum Light

A full-spectrum light for a 20-gallon container should cost $13.00 or £10 and the fixture for it should cost $17.00 or £13. A dual full-spectrum light with daytime and nighttime bulbs with a stand should cost $85.00 or £66.

Incandescent Light Bulb

This should cost $5.00 or £4 and a quality safe fixture again will depend if you will use a clamp-on type ($12.00 or £9).

Chapter 4. Turtles Living With Tortoises

Tortoises are not the easiest animals to keep. They grow much larger than most turtle species and need a great deal of space. They are also very sensitive to their environments. Ideally, tortoises should live outdoors, in a pen. Different species of tortoise have very distinct requirements, which can make outdoor or indoor living a challenge.

There are some general divisions of tortoises: Mediterranean, African Savannah, South American/Tropical, Temperate, and Desert. It is not easy to provide the proper habitat for a tortoise unless you happen to live in a climate very close to the one that species comes from. Tropical tortoises require proper humidity, something difficult to duplicate when you live in Arizona, for example. Temperate tortoises are hardier and can hibernate outside if they have the right setup, or hibernate in a container (see Hibernation in the care chapter). Desert tortoises have a very hard time adapting to life in a humid climate, such as Virginia. When choosing a tortoise, if you select one from a similar climate to your own, it will make keeping your pet happy and healthy that much easier.

In addition to space and climate issues, you must be concerned about providing the proper substrate. Tortoises rely just as much on the right substrate as turtles rely on clean water. Tortoises dig in their substrate, burrow in it, and use it to regulate their body temperature. The wrong substrate can contribute to huge health problems in these animals.

Unfortunately, there are plenty of problematic substrates sold for use with tortoises. Do NOT use the following as substrates for your tortoise:
1) Pine and cedar shavings: Causes respiratory problems in nearly every species of small animal living on them. Heat from the basking

lamp causes fumes from the wood oils, and can cause intestinal problems if eaten.

2) Calcium sand: Marketed as an ideal reptile substrate, it can cause dehydration in tortoises, irritated eyes, and intestinal problems.

3) Bark mulch: Similar problems as wood shavings. Also popular with parasites that want to live with tortoises. Note: This is not typically a problem with cypress or orchid barks and mulches.

4) Coconut and other fibers: Problems with dust, growing bacteria, and contributing to dehydration. Doesn't help with temperature regulation.

5) Alfalfa pellets: Can contribute to dehydration and infections, too much protein if eaten regularly.

6) Newspaper and paper towels: No burrowing available for tortoises, and can catch fire.

Now that you know what to avoid, let's look at good substrates for tortoises:

a) Top soil: Don't confuse this with potting soil, which often contains fertilizers, which might be swallowed, etc. A good loamy top soil is very comfortable as a base for many tortoises, and is good to burrow in.

b) Sand: Play sand that you would use in a child's sand box is a very good substrate for burrowing. It drains off excess water well, so it's very useful in habitats for dry-climate tortoises.

c) Sphagnum peat moss: An excellent addition to top soil for tortoises that need humidity. Comfortable for burrowing and keeps moisture in the habitat.

d) Orchid or Cypress bark or mulch: Mix into soil or distribute on top of other substrates. Excellent for increasing humidity.

The experts at Tortoise Trust have done a great deal of testing on different substrates, and they recommend a mixture of loamy top soil and sand for all tortoises. The trick is to adjust the mixture to meet the needs of different species. For example, tortoises that prefer more humidity, such as Turtles and Red-footed Tortoises, would need more loam than sand in the mix (the recommendation is around 60% loam, 40% sand), plus some peat moss for additional moisture. An African Spurred Tortoise or Desert Tortoise would need far more sand, perhaps 70% sand with 30% loam mixed in, with no peat moss. The result is a substrate that is safe to use, gives tortoises what they need, and is far less expensive than what you would spend for commercially-produced substrates. This is ideal to use in both indoor and outdoor living situations.

Indoor Living

Keeping a tortoise indoors is tricky, primarily because these animals require so much floor space. While turtles get most of their exercise by swimming, tortoises require room to walk around without having to go in circles because their enclosure is too small. And yes, you can get by with a smaller area while the animal is a hatchling or juvenile, but it doesn't take more than three or four years before your African Spurred Tortoise weighs nearly 50 pounds and is on his way to weighing twice that.

If you must house your tortoise indoors, either during the cooler months of the year or because you don't have any outdoor options available, you should expect to dedicate an entire room to your pet. With the larger species, this option will not last more than a few years before the tortoise is far too big for a single room. If you have more than one connecting room or a large area in the basement you can dedicate to a larger tortoise, indoor living is possible, as long as you provide proper lighting, heating, substrate, etc. However, for most people, donating that much square footage to their pet is unacceptable.

Large tortoises produce much more waste than smaller species do. Daily cleaning is often the price you pay to keep your entire home from smelling like your tortoise's habitat. Many keepers build a separate "tortoise house" in their yard, a dedicated building with the proper habitat setup for their pet, rather than bring the tortoise into their own home. Hatchlings will usually do all right in a 50-gallon stock tank or Rubbermaid container. Juvenile tortoises, or adults of smaller species, can be adequately housed in either a dedicated room (fenced near the door so you can get in and out of the room without stepping on or hitting a tortoise with the door), or in a tortoise table.

While there are many different ways to build a tortoise table, the basic concept is the same:
1) A plywood (usually ¾" thick) floor.
2) Plexiglass or wood sides, at least 18" high to discourage climbing and escapes. If you use Plexiglass, be sure to paint or otherwise cover the outside, at least to above the tortoise's eye level, because tortoises will try to break through what they can see through.
c) A shallow tray, such as one used in photo developing, for water.
d) Deeper trays, such as those used for cat litter, for holding substrate and plants.
e) Lighting and basking lamps, as mentioned in the section above. Take care to provide varying temperatures in the habitat, so the tortoise can regulate its body temperature.
f) Appropriate substrate.

You may cut holes in the plywood floor to enable the trays to settle into the floor. You may also want to leave the trays on top of the floor, and add substrate all around the trays, up to the lid. Most keepers choose the in-the-floor option because it makes the habitat easier to clean and maintain.
Some keepers build ramps and a secondary level for basking, while adding substrate below that level for a dark burrow. Others provide boxes for cover or piles of peat moss for burrowing. For tortoises that need humidity, the table can be partially covered and misters used to increase the moisture in the air.

Outdoor Living

Obviously, providing enough space is important when creating an outdoor environment for your tortoise. Whether you live in the appropriate climate for your tortoise to live outside year-round, or you are creating a summer-only pen, here are things to consider:

Size

Bigger is better. Some experts recommend at least 10 square feet per 6" of turtle length, others suggest no less than 30 square feet. In general, devote as much space to your tortoise as you can, and if you get a species that will grow huge, such as an African Spurred or Leopard Tortoise, you might want to just donate your backyard to the tortoise.

Substrate

Take out the lovely green grass growing in the area where your tortoise will live. Grass creates a mini climate that is too humid and cool for most tortoises. So remove the grass, and add appropriate sand or loam or peat to create the proper substrate for your tortoise. Try to alter the surface of the ground so it isn't flat, creating gentle slopes and varied terrain for a more natural, interesting environment.

Enclosure

There are two things to remember when creating the enclosure for your tortoise. First, tortoises will try to get through fences if they can see through them, whether by pushing through or digging under. Second, tortoises can be very good climbers and escape by going up and over your fence, especially if there are square corners for the tortoise to climb. So it is much better to have a rounded perimeter rather than a square or rectangle one.

For the best results, build a sturdy fence of wood (NOT pressure or rot treated with chemicals) or vinyl that the tortoise cannot see through. Dig a trench where the fence will be placed and set concrete blocks below the fence, 6"-12" into the ground, to discourage digging under the fence by both tortoises and external predators. To better protect your tortoise from predators, cover the enclosure with wire netting.

Water
Tap water is usually fine for tortoises, unless you have really bad water that is heavily chlorinated. If you have a commercial filter on your tap already, the water will be fine. If you're concerned about the water, you can use an animal-safe conditioner designed to neutralize the water, such as ReptiSafe. Make sure the water tray is one your tortoise can climb out of easily, and that you change the water at least daily.

Basking spots and shade
Your tortoise will change positions throughout the day to regulate its temperature, so you need to provide areas that are warmer and cooler. A basking spot can be a clearing, free of vegetation, under a suspended basking lamp if necessary to reach the proper level of heat. Shade can be provided with boxes and taller plants. Check thermometers to be sure you have a range of temperatures throughout the enclosure.

Other furnishings
Tortoises are busy creatures. They may spend time basking, but they do a fair amount of wandering, grazing, and snooping around. Make their habitat interesting by providing gently varied heights in the terrain, plenty of places to hide and explore, rocks, logs, etc. Many keepers provide a small shed or doghouse that is heated for nighttime and bad weather. Be creative when you decorate your pet's enclosure. If you use furnishings to break up the view, create false walls, etc., your tortoise will be more distracted from thoughts of escape.

Plants
Adding the right plants to your turtle's enclosure will provide shade, hiding places, and food, as well as look better than bare substrate.

One particularly good idea is to concentrate the plants toward the middle of the enclosure, to keep your tortoise's attention away from the walls.

Some excellent plants to include for your tortoise's grazing pleasure include:
1) Aloe
2) Bermuda Grass
3) Buffalo Grass
4) Dandelions
5) Fescue
6) Geraniums
7) Grapes
8) Hibiscus
9) Honeysuckle
10) Kale
11) Pansies
12) Prickly Pear
13) Rosemary
14) Roses
15) Thyme
16) Tall grasses such as Pampas
17) Wildflowers

Some common plants may look good in your tortoise's habitat but are actually toxic. This is not a complete list, but plants to watch out for include:
a) Azalea
b) Boxwood
c) Creeping Charlie
d) Daffodils
e) Foxgloves
f) Holly
g) Hyacinth
h) Ivy

i) Juniper

j) Marigolds

k) Morning Glory

l) Periwinkle

m) Rhododendron

n) Shasta Daisies

Lighting

One of the best parts of outdoor living is the unfiltered sunlight that helps your tortoise generate the vitamin D3 it needs. You may still need a basking lamp or two, but these can be standard incandescent basking bulbs.

Chapter 5. Feeding and Diet

All turtles and tortoises do not eat the same things. Some are strict carnivores, some are vegetarians. Some will eat anything. In the species specifics section, each species will be identified as a carnivore, omnivore, or herbivore, with notes on food items in addition to the ones described here, if necessary.
Let's look at the basic food requirements of carnivores, herbivores and omnivores in the chelonian world.

Carnivores
Owning a carnivorous turtle is a great way to deal with the pests in your garden, assuming you don't apply pesticides and herbicides to the areas where you're collecting them. Slugs, snails, grasshoppers, and crickets are all excellent foods for these turtles. Earthworms are often a favorite food, as are feeder fish. Mealworms are good, as well as pinkie mice. Many turtles are fond of crayfish, but it's best to get these from a store, or be sure to freeze them for a month or so if you catch them yourself. Otherwise parasites may be passed to your turtle.

You can also feed such things as beef, chicken, and turkey. While some keepers say raw is fine, poultry is best fed after being cooked and cooled. Turtles have enough trouble with salmonella naturally; they don't need additional sources in their food. Commercial turtle pellet food has come a long way in the last couple of decades and is a decent base for a turtle's diet, but it should never completely replace fresh food. ReptoMin, Mazuri, Rep-Cal, and Zoo Med (the varieties formulated for carnivores) are highly recommended by many turtle experts. Some of these brands even offer food in smaller sizes for hatchlings.

It's also a good idea to offer greens (not fruit) to carnivorous turtles, because most will turn into omnivores as they age.

Herbivores

Tortoises are almost always vegetarians, and while it would seem that this would make feeding them much easier than feeding carnivores, the opposite is true. The trouble with tortoises is that their diet requirements can vary widely, depending on their native environment. In the habitats section, you learned about the different needs of Mediterranean, African Savannah, Tropical, Temperate, and Desert Tortoises. The dietary needs for these animals break down along similar lines. Herbivorous diets are not one-size-fits-all. Like other herbivores, these animals tend to eat by grazing throughout the day. If your tortoise is housed outdoors, planting their enclosure with appropriate vegetation that they can munch on is an excellent idea. You can then supplement with calcium-dusted fruits (if appropriate for the species) and vegetables.

A.C. Highfield, an expert from Tortoise Trust, warns against the use of commercial turtle food for herbivores. "We have tested most of these products over the years, and in our view, they should be avoided. We have also seen numerous 'dietary disasters' attributable to their use." Highfield notes that pellets designed for herbivores tend to contain far too much protein and sugar. "Our advice is simple. We see no need for these commercial feeding products and we believe their use is unsafe . . . We strongly recommend that you avoid them."

For all tortoises, it's best to avoid feeding too many "grocery store greens." Red-leaf lettuce and endive are a suitable supplement to the plants you'll use in your pet's enclosure, and squash is a nice treat on occasion. Too much of these and foods like tomatoes, which are full of water, tend to cause loose stools and digestive problems.

As a general rule, tortoises need high fiber in their diets. Mediterranean tortoises enjoy leaves and flowers, and African savannah tortoises are fond of grasses. Tropical tortoises and wood turtles are more omnivorous and can be fed fruit and some animal protein. All tortoises can benefit from eating grass or timothy hay. Alfalfa hay offers excellent calcium, but is also high in protein, so other hays are better. Certain vegetables and greens contain acids and tannins that can cause problems for your tortoise. It's a good idea to avoid feeding beans, cabbage, chard, corn or spinach. Mustard or collard greens can be used on occasion.

Omnivores

In the wild, meat is much harder to come by. If your turtle can get meat, it will take it, no matter how much vegetation is available to eat. This makes feeding omnivorous turtles a bit tricky. It is up to you to not provide too much meat, or your turtle will only want to eat meat and will develop health problems because of it. Remember, even carnivorous turtles frequently turn more herbivorous as adults.

Ideally, omnivores should be allowed to graze or be provided with vegetation only for most meals. Dandelions, watercress, collard greens, mustard greens, squash, and kale are good items for an omnivore's diet. Meat should be provided sparingly. Regardless of whether you're feeding a carnivore, herbivore, or omnivore, variety is imperative for balanced nutrition. Don't rely on feeding just one kind of food, even if it is your pet's favorite, or your chelonian will experience nutritional deficiencies and health problems.

Feeding intervals and amounts

Turtles and tortoises can be difficult to feed. They may be very picky, so it takes a while for you to learn what they like and what they don't. They are also constantly on the hunt for food, even when they aren't really hungry. Once they learn that you provide food, these animals often learn to beg for extra treats or meals. Don't fall for it. Overfeeding is every bit as dangerous to chelonians as underfeeding. Unfortunately, this creates a dilemma for chelonian keepers. How do you know how much food to provide and how often? The best thing to do is decide on a scheduled feeding time and don't provide food at any other time. That way your animal won't be overfed. Feeding on a schedule will also encourage your pet to eat when food is given, because it will be hungry.

Feeding is not an exact science, but most experts recommend feeding hatchlings and juveniles every day, and adults every other day or three times per week. Some recommend having greens available at all times and supplementing with commercial foods, meats or fruit (for some species) every day for hatchlings, every other day for juveniles and two or three times per week for adults. Others suggest offering a snack between meal times but not leaving any food lying around between meals (this is primarily with turtles). The best thing to do is to use these recommendations as a starting place, then develop your own methods as you care for your pet.

The amount of food to offer can be controversial as well. Some chelonian specialists suggest feeding as much as your turtle or tortoise will eat in a 15 minute period, then removing the rest of the food. Others recommend feeding until the animal has eaten an amount that would fit inside its head (if it were hollow) and no more. Others suggest letting a chelonian eat until it slows down, then removing the food. Whichever method you choose, remember overfeeding can be harmful, so letting an animal gorge itself is not a good idea.

Supplements
There is a debate in the world of chelonian enthusiasts between the need for supplements and the need to go "natural". Vitamin A is a particular problem, because too little causes health issues, but too much will cause additional problems, such as peeling skin. Vitamin D3 can be supplemented, but it is better to let the turtle or tortoise synthesize its own D3 through exposure to sunlight or a UVB light in their habitat.
Calcium is one supplement that everyone agrees should be given. Some recommend leaving a cuttlebone, such as those used for pet birds, in the enclosure. Your pet can chew on it as desired. You'll

want to dust your pet's food with calcium carbonate powder at least twice a week, though many keepers do so as often as every feeding. Your vet can give you more firm direction on supplementing your pet, based on its health and individual needs.

A word about dog food
Actually, this applies to cat food as well. A surprising number of chelonian keepers give their pets canned dog or cat food, but this is not a good idea, except as an occasional treat. These foods are too high in protein and fats to be a staple in a chelonian's diet.

Water
Turtles drink while swimming, another reason to make sure the water stays clean. Tortoises should always have a shallow bowl or tray of clean water they can easily climb in and out of, in order to drink and soak as they please. This means you'll be changing the water often, at least daily.

Insects
If you have a young turtle, or if you are breeding turtles, you will definitely want to provide them with a readily available supply of insects to eat. As I mentioned earlier in the book, young turtles will eat mostly insects when they are growing because of the protein needed to develop. However, unlike a lot of other reptiles that should eat a mainly herbivorous diet, turtles can eat insects throughout their whole lives without any real issues arising.

The best and easiest thing to feed your turtle insect-wise are things like snails, slugs, grasshoppers, earthworms, crickets, wax worms, cicadas, sow bugs and mealworms. Turtles absolutely love mealworms, so you shouldn't have any problems getting them to start feeding on mealworms right away.

Sometimes turtles do take a little while to get settled in to their new surroundings and feel comfortable, so sometimes they won't eat right away. If this does happen, just give it some time and keep trying each day and within a week you should have some success. Some people also feed low-fat dog food with great success. Just make sure you only feed the low-fat varieties and not high-fat cat foods, as too much fat can lead to Steatitis or fatty liver issues.

Vegetables, Salad and Fruits
As with most reptiles, you can feed turtles a wide variety of greens and vegetables. However, you should definitely avoid feeding them broccoli and spinach, as both of these foods will block calcium absorption. We recommend feeding strawberries, apple, banana, mushrooms, pear and green-leafed vegetables. Most turtles will eat the salad and vegetables willingly, however some are bit more picky. They may be unwilling to break their early eating habits and will only really want to eat insects.

I great tip to get your turtles eating vegetables is to trick them into thinking they are eating a mealworm. Turtles aren't the brightest animals in the world so it's actually pretty easy to do this. All you need to do is cut some vegetables into meal worm sized strips (this works particularly well with apple).

Next, hold a mealworm in your hand and show it to your turtle. When the mealworm starts wriggling about in front of it, your turtle should open its mouth ready to eat, at this point you simply have the mealworm shaped strip of apple in your other hand and you put it up to its mouth. It will bite without thinking twice and they will usually eat the whole strip right away.

Sometimes, when the turtle has noticed that it's not moving, it will stop eating. This is when you need to re-engage the sneaky tactics and wriggle it with your fingers. As soon as they see it moving they should have another bite.

Try changing things up and using different vegetables. If you keep doing this, before long your turtle will be used to eating vegetables and will eat them willingly without having to go through the trickery process each time.

How Much Should It Eat?

A quick and easy rule for knowing how much you should feed your turtle is that you should feed the same amount of food as the size of their head. So try to imagine how much food would fit in their head if it was hollow! That's roughly how much they should be eating each day.

This is due to some pretty simple logic. A turtle's head is about the same size as its stomach, so there you have it!

Supplements

Vitamin supplements are a great idea to keep your turtles in the best health possible and ensure they have all of the vitamins and nutrients that they require.

Vitamin-A deficiency and calcium deficiency are both common problems in turtles. Some kind of multi-vitamin and a calcium supplement added to the turtle's food a couple of times a week will help a great deal to help prevent these issues from arising. You can find specialist supplements online and in specialist pet stores without too much difficulty. There are some brands that actually provide specialist turtle supplement powders which work great. All you do is simply sprinkle the recommended amount over their food.

As I mentioned before, turtles require a good amount of vitamin-A in their diet. Although the supplement powder will most probably contain a good amount of vitamin A, a great way to make sure they are getting enough is to simply add a light drizzle of cod liver oil to their food a couple of times a week. Don't worry about giving them slightly too much, it's better than them not getting enough and it would be very hard to make them sick by overdosing them on it.

A Note on Outdoor Enclosures

Something we felt necessary to add to this feeding section is that, in an outdoor enclosure, insects will more than likely come passing through regularly. This will give your turtles a readily available supply of food that they can hunt in a very natural way. This is fantastic for your turtles as it will give them a varied diet and make things a bit more enjoyable for them, as they will get to hunt in a more natural and instinctive way. For adult turtles, these random insects will probably provide all of the protein they need. So you can just feed them their vegetables along with their supplements and not have to worry too much about feeding them mealworms and other insects. When you water the enclosure to keep the humidity up, this will draw worms up to the surface and attract slugs, which the turtles will snap up readily.

Fasting

Turtles have a quite worrying trait; they will sometimes decide not to eat for extended periods of time for no apparent reason. If you notice that you have a turtle that hasn't eaten for over a week, it's best to seek advice from a local veterinarian, but it's usually nothing to worry about and they will start eating again of their own accord. This fasting could possibly be attributed to being too cold. Their bodies and metabolism will slow down as they get colder and so they will eat less. This is perfectly normal as the weather starts to get cold, however if you have indoor turtles, check your vivarium temperatures to make sure everything is in order.

Meeting Your Turtle's Nutritional Needs

It isn't enough to provide your turtle with a spacious enclosure that is well-regulated and well-maintained. If you want to keep your Turtle healthy and thriving, you also have to provide them with a well-balanced diet.

Turtles can be a finicky lot to feed – and this can sometimes be worrying because many turtles can suffer from chronic nutritional problems while in captivity. In the wild, they don't have the luxury of being picky about their food because of the natural seasonal changes they go through, and for this reason they are considered opportunistic eaters that eat pretty much whatever food they come across.

Such is no longer true for turtles raised in captivity, and so poor nutrition is a very real danger. It is therefore extremely essential that you provide your turtle with a varied diet that provides them with as much of their nutritional needs as possible. Occasional variations can help entice even picky turtles to keep eating, but the nutritional value should always be present to help maintain your turtle's optimal health.

The Nutritional Needs of Turtles

Turtles are omnivores, which means that they eat both plants and animal-based foods. While they can eat just about anything, it is highly recommended that they be fed only foods that they would naturally come across in the wild – and that means avoiding artificial or man-made foods such as chips, hot dogs, cheese, bread, candy, etc. Doing so can only increase the fussiness of your turtle's choices in their food.

As a general guideline, their diet can be broken down as an equal 50% plant-based food, and 50% animal-based food. As already mentioned, depending on their life stage this does vary somewhat. Turtles up to 4-6 years of age seem to primarily be carnivores, while adult turtles tend to be more herbivorous. At all times, they should have easy access to clean and fresh drinking water. Please consult with your veterinarian regarding the best diet plan for your turtle.

Animal or high-protein foods

You will probably want to explore a wide variety of protein-based food sources for your turtle, which could include earthworms, caterpillars, mealworms, wax worms, wax worms, snails, slugs, moths, spiders, grasshoppers, crickets, beetles and even pinkies (or baby mice). Insects may not provide your turtle with enough calcium, so you will probably want to enrich their meal with calcium supplements such as powdered calcium carbonate, lactate, citrate, or gluconate. Dust the insect with these before feeding them to the turtle.

Occasionally, you might want to shake things up by giving them vitamin-fortified chows, but this should in no instance exceed 5% of the turtle's total diet. Commercial reptile pets can be an excellent source of protein, but it is always a good idea to offer them live food more often than food that is commercially bought. If you offer them dry feed or pellets, soak these in water for 30 minutes to soften them.

A word of warning regarding collecting various insects for food – avoid collecting them from your home garden as much as possible. It is preferential to raise them yourself or to buy them from pet stores, bait stores, or reptile breeders. This caution is to avoid collecting insects or slugs that have been exposed to fertilizers, insecticides or any other chemicals that may be harmful to your turtle.

Plant-based food, including fruits and vegetables
While plant-based food should comprise at least 50% of your turtle's diet, you should offer them more vegetables than fruits – the latter should not be more than 10-20% of this portion. Fruits can entice your turtle's taste buds, but they can also be mineral deficient. On the other hand, they get more nutritional value from leafy greens, so these should be fed more liberally.

Some of the fruits turtles are fond of include strawberries, tomatoes, apples, grapes, cherries, pears, kiwi, oranges, figs, melons, bananas, mangoes, grapefruit, raspberries, peaches, pears, plums, and nectarines.

Dark, leafy green vegetables are highly recommended for turtles, and these can include cabbage, spinach, romaine lettuce, broccoli, squash, sweet potatoes, carrots, beets, pea pods, and mushrooms. Be careful when feeding your turtle mushrooms – avoid the toxic or poisonous kind, especially if you are gathering many of your turtle's food from the wild. Occasionally, you may wish to offer your turtle treats in the form of edible flowers such as carnations, dandelions, hibiscus, nasturtiums and geraniums.

Important Vitamins and Minerals

Vitamin A – Vitamin A rich foods include yellow or dark orange vegetables, dark and leafy green vegetables, and liver (for instance, from whole mice).

Vitamin D3 – This is usually sourced from sunlight or any other UVB producing light source. Vitamin D3 helps your turtle in the conversion of calcium into usable compounds, and so most calcium supplements recommended for turtles also contain Vitamin D3.

Calcium – Turtles need a high dose of calcium, and many veterinarians recommend supplementing their dietary calcium. A light sprinkling of calcium powder (such as calcium gluconate, lactate, or carbonate) over their regular food can be done each week. Be careful, however, about over-supplementation. Always consult your veterinarian before giving your turtle any supplement.

Fiber – Not getting enough fiber can be unhealthy for your turtle's digestive system, and that is why providing them with a healthy portion of leafy greens in their diet is important. In the wild, turtles usually get their fiber from eating leaves and grasses.

Phosphorous – While turtles need phosphorous in their diet, this is already usually found in abundance in the usual foods they eat. It is highly recommended that any calcium supplements you provide your turtle should be those that do not contain phosphorous.

Water – Turtles need fresh, clean water at all times – not only for drinking, but also for soaking. Dehydration is a very real danger, especially for turtles kept in captivity, and regular misting is recommended on top of the daily supply of fresh water. Offer your turtle its clean, fresh water in a clean, shallow dish or pan that will not be easily overturned, and with a kind of "ramp" along the sides so that your turtle can easily climb in and out of its own accord. Make sure that the water level does not reach higher than its chin, or else you are also running the risk of your turtle drowning. Turtles often defecate or pee in their water bowls, too – so it is imperative that their water dish be cleaned regularly to avoid contamination or infections. Always remember to wash your hands carefully after handling any of your turtle's equipment.

Tips for Feeding Your Turtle

One of the key ways of dealing with Turtles that are also finicky eaters is to provide them with as much variety as possible. Many suggest avoiding giving your turtle the same food twice in a row – this can grow into an "addiction" or "fixation" for a particular food or taste, and can be very difficult to break later on. Turtles seem to be particularly attracted to red, yellow and orange foods in addition to live, moving food. You can try cutting up or chopping fruits, vegetables and insects and mixing them together to better entice them to eat, while also providing them with a healthy and balanced meal.

Feed your turtle according to their natural daily rhythm. In the wild, turtles are most active during the early morning or late afternoon, when the sun is not too hot. Their activity also increases when it rains, so this is a good time to feed them when you are keeping them in an outdoor enclosure. If they are kept indoors, misting or spraying the cage with water can help stimulate their appetite.

Wash the fruits and vegetables, then chop them into small, bite-sized pieces for easier feeding. Greater variety in the foods you feed your turtle can help ensure a healthy and balanced diet. Offer these to your turtle in a shallow dish that will not be easily overturned. Occasionally, you may wish to offer them their food on top of a flat rock which they can easily climb. This more natural approach will also help maintain their beaks and toenails from becoming overgrown.

Feed adults three or more times per week, or every other day, in the morning. Juveniles and growing turtles should be fed daily.

If you are keeping your turtle indoors, occasionally bringing them out for exposure to real sunlight may help improve their appetite.

You can also try some variety in where you feed them if you are having a difficult time getting them to eat – some turtles do prefer a bit more privacy while feeding, so offering them food in a more sheltered area may be more enticing for them than right out in the open.

If you find your turtle fixating on a particular food while also refusing to eat anything else, try mixing up their favourite food with the new food, chopping each finely to encourage them not to discriminate too much.

If your turtle refuses to eat for more than two weeks, seek veterinary care. Sometimes their refusal to eat can be caused by a medical problem or eating disorder.

Chapter 6. Turtle Care and Husbandry

One of the keys to caring for your turtle is learning as much as you can about their life and their behavior in the wild, and approximating this as closely as possible even in captive conditions. This entails doing a lot of independent research – focusing particularly on the type of turtle you are, or are planning on, keeping. Naturally, the specific needs of each turtle change depending on the type – which is essentially based on their region of origin. This means also learning as much as you can about the natural seasons, weather, climate, flora and fauna of your turtle's native region.

Turtle Hibernation or Brumation

Also depending on their region of origin and the seasons, turtles are known for hibernating during the winter months – a process that is also sometimes referred to as brumation. This can last for 3-5 months, depending on the prevailing weather conditions. In regions where there is no true winter, turtles may only slow down during the cooler winter months and not enter a true hibernation state at all.

Hibernation itself is triggered by a decrease in daylight hours and lowering temperatures. During these colder months and severe decrease in temperatures, given their dependence on external factors for internal temperature regulation, these adaptable turtles will dig in deep into the soil or substrate, looking for safer temperatures where they can maintain themselves in extreme conditions. Hibernating turtles in the wild are essentially unprotected, and many can die during this period – whether due to harsh weather conditions or because they have become vulnerable to predators.

It is interesting to note that brumating or hibernating reptiles or turtles also require this period to prepare for breeding – during this cooling period, ovulation is stimulated, as well as the production of sperm. Unless you are fully intending on breeding your turtle, you might want to keep your turtles carefully separated when they come out of hibernation during the spring months, or you might find yourself responsible for a nest of eggs that will soon be living, thriving hatchlings!

Because hibernation or brumation is essentially dependent on external environmental conditions, many turtle owners deliberate each time during the winter months whether or not they should even hibernate their turtle at all. Turtles living in captive conditions are essentially also living in artificial conditions, which means that outdoor seasonal changes need not affect your yurtle too much. In certain instances, it may not be advisable to hibernate your turtle – for instance, if you have not had your turtle for more than a year, when their health is in a poor condition, or when you do not have access to, or have not been able to prepare, a proper hibernation place for your turtle (a particular concern for turtles kept in outdoor enclosures).

On the other hand, hibernation or brumation is an essential part of a turtle's growth and development – this helps them maintain normal thyroid activities and complete normal life expectancies. Hibernation also helps them synchronize their reproduction cycles and prepare for breeding and reproduction, but this can also be a dangerous time for the turtle, as this is a period of time when the turtle's biological processes are barely working to keep them alive, including their immune system. An inappropriately chosen place for hibernation could also endanger them, whether due to flooding and eventual drowning, dehydration, freezing to death, or becoming vulnerable to predators.

A good rule of thumb is not to hibernate if your veterinarian finds something wrong with your turtle health-wise.

Preparing a Hibernaculum
In the wild, turtles hibernate at temperatures below 50°F, and hibernation periods generally begin at around mid-October. If you

want your turtle to hibernate outdoors, you should prepare them a safe and protected place they can burrow into during the winter months – preferably under a mound of leaves or other protective covers such as logs or rocks. The ground should be prepared so that they could go as deeply as they need to go; some have been found to burrow to depths of at least 2 feet. You can then protect them from the possibility of drowning by protecting this area from rain or flooding by providing a waterproof cover. You should, however, make sure that they have ready access to clean drinking water in case they should surface for a drink.

Please remember that the turtles are very defenseless during this time, which means that unless you can guarantee their protection against roaming predators and other natural dangers, you should probably prepare an indoor hibernaculum for them instead, or simply not have them hibernate at all.

Turtles that are kept primarily indoors throughout the year might require a bit more preparation for brumation. Ceasing to feed them 2-3 weeks prior to hibernation will alert their bodies to the natural food scarcity that takes place during winter. Allowing them to soak in tepid water will keep them hydrated and will also encourage elimination. This is important because undigested food left in their system can cause them severe illnesses over the following months. Feed them high-fiber foods prior to this time to promote elimination.

Then begin to bring down the temperature in their enclosure by increments of some 5 degrees each time to allow it to acclimate to cooler temperatures. It is best to bring them to a vet for a checkup to ensure that its physical health is sufficient to carry it through hibernation conditions. Some owners use the refrigeration method to help mimic the natural conditions of lower winter temperatures. The important thing is not to completely close or seal up the fridge door so as to maintain oxygen and breathing requirements.

If you do wish for your turtle to hibernate indoors, prepare a suitable place for them to do so. This is called a hibernaculum or a hibernation box, and is the preferred method for turtles hibernating in areas to which they are not native, and for owners who wish to have greater control over the external conditions of their turtle's brumation.

Prepare a container and fill this with moist peat moss and newspaper. You can either leave this uncovered or place a lid on it with appropriately drilled holes. Once your turtle begins to slow down, place it into the smaller container and keep it in an area with a steady temperature ranging from 45-50°F in a draft-free room. Humidity levels should also be maintained. Be sure to set aside clean water for your turtle in case it surfaces for a drink. Even for indoor hibernation boxes, you should ensure that your turtle is be kept safe from the dangers of foraging creatures, including fire ants. Check up on your hibernating turtle periodically during the next 2-3 months – make sure that your turtle is properly hydrated, looks healthy, and is still hibernating. The substrate should be clean and free of molds. Change it if necessary, or hydrate it again if it has become too dry. If your turtle has already become too active, or wakes up too often to look for a drink, it's possible that it may be sick. If so, you should bring it out of hibernation early and allow it to overwinter indoors. This entails gradually bringing up their core body temperature, regular feeding, and keeping it in warm and high humidity conditions.

To bring your turtle out of hibernation, the temperature should be gradually increased to 60°F degrees for around two days, then to room temperature, then to their normal environmental conditions. Soak them every other day, and begin feeding them around two days after they have been returned to normal room temperatures. Be aware, though, that some turtles may not eat for some time – and certain males may not eat at all until after breeding.

Chapter 7. Turtle Handling and Temperament

Many turtle hobbyists and keepers will be quick to tell you that keeping one for a pet can be incredibly boring. You feed your turtle, you clean up after them, make sure they are safe and healthy and have everything they need, and they hardly demonstrate any affection or gratitude for all your efforts. Some days, you might not even catch a glimpse of them if they're feeling particularly private. Does that seem contrary to everything that a pet is supposed to be? Like with most reptiles, one should come to terms with the fact that turtles make beautiful but rather indifferent pets – quite different from their portrayal in cartoons and animated movies or films.

Still, keeping one as a pet involves the occasional physical contact with your turtle. It bears stressing that excessive handling can cause your pet turtle undue stress, and should be avoided when it is unnecessary to handle them in the first place. If you really do need to pick them up and handle them, for instance when you are checking their physical health, preparing to bring them to a vet, or need to move them so that you can give their enclosure a thorough cleaning, there are a few crucial things you need to remember.

Turtle Temperament
Turtles are attractive, fairly hardy, and intelligent animals. The temperament varies individually and by type, but in general, turtles are gentle and mellow creatures. Their name derives from their ability to retract completely within their shell, using the hinged plastron on their carapace. They typically grow to a moderate size of 4-7 inches, and live for approximately 40-50 years. They make great first time turtle pets, although they are still considered high maintenance pets.

If you are considering bringing home a turtle as a pet, please do extensive research beforehand to make sure that you are capable of giving them the long-term care that they need. It is advisable to purchase or adopt only turtles that have been bred in captivity, rather than those captured from the wild. The latter may be illegal in certain states, as turtles that have lived and survived in the wild can become extremely stressed when thrown into a new and strange environment.

Turtles are known for being attached to their region of origin, and they do not like being transplanted completely into strange new surroundings. Doing so may only severely shorten their lifespan. Not to mention the fact that wild caught turtles may carry parasites or bacteria that can be extremely harmful to humans.

Of course, even turtles raised and bred in captivity have the same attachment to familiar surroundings, and they will also suffer stress and anxiety when thrown into a completely new environment – regardless of how beautiful the enclosure you prepared for it is. Turtles bred in captivity have been known to be gentler in temperament, and are at least more familiar with the comings and goings of humans in their immediate surroundings.

Turtles are fairly hardy, but they can also be pretty delicate in terms of their constitution. As long as you provide them with a well-maintained and clean enclosure, and provide them a fresh supply of clean water and a well-balanced diet, illnesses and sicknesses can be kept to a minimum. It is always a good idea, however, to research the local vets in your area and find one that has experience in dealing with reptiles so that you know where to go in case of a medical emergency.

Tips for Handling your Turtle
Caution in handling your turtle serves two purposes: it prevents you from causing your pet turtle any injury or undue stress, and also protects you from being attacked by your turtle (yes, it can happen),

or from being infected with any dangerous bacteria or diseases that turtles may carry.

Always remember to wash your hands thoroughly after handling your turtle or any of their equipment such as their cage, dishes, or any of the plants, rocks, substratum, and other components of their enclosure. Doing so can help prevent the possibility of disease transmissions from any bacteria that your pet turtle may be carrying.

Many turtles grown and raised in captivity can become responsive to the presence of their keepers, though this is probably because they are equating your presence to that of being fed. Unlike turtles in the wild that shy away from human contact, some acclimated turtles will eagerly position themselves to meet you when you come and feed them.

In general, however, turtles do not like being handled, and even tame ones react negatively to being picked up and raised off of the ground. While this may sometimes be necessary during routine cage maintenance, for example, such handling should be kept to a minimum if at all possible. Turtles should not be handled by children or people with low immunity – if this cannot be avoided, there should be very close supervision.

Smaller turtles can be lifted with the fingers and thumb, and lifted by placing them on your open palm. They should always be restrained, however, in order to prevent their scrambling off and possibly injuring themselves by a fall. Larger turtles, on the other hand, should be grasped by both hands, one hand on each side of its shell. Be careful because some of them may react strongly by kicking or scratching. Try not to cause your turtle any scratches or injure its shell. Any injury they suffer, whether on their shell or otherwise, could possibly become infected. Remember that the turtle's shell is also a living and growing part of your turtle's physical make-up, and is not impervious to feeling. If you do get scratched yourself, the wounds should be sterilized before being dressed.

Needless to say, always ensure that you do not drop your turtle. This can cause them severe injury for which a vet's services should be sought immediately.

The Growth and Development of Turtles

A turtle's skin is not like the skin of humans or animals, which stretch and grow to accommodate one's growth. Their skin is more leathery, tough, and may look like it is covered by small scales. Periodically, he will outgrow his skin, and as he does so, he sheds the old skin and leaves it behind. This is also true for their shell, in order to allow for their growth in size. But they also do this in order to prevent potential health risks such as infections that can come from shell rot or other parasitic infections that may have taken hold on its shell.

A turtle's body is covered by skin, and a shell that is made mostly of bone. This shell is fused to his body, and its outside is layered in plates or scales that are called scutes that cover and protect the bones and cartilage of the shell underneath. Scutes are akin to fingernails, and are made of the same substance called keratin. Your turtle will occasionally shed its skin, but it will shed its scutes more often. When this happens, the scutes peel or flake off piece by piece and are replaced by new ones.

Turtles will shed when needed in order to prevent shell rot and infection – and this can happen if the turtle has soaked for too long in water, and is unable to dry itself off effectively. These conditions are potential risks for shell rot, but in general, turtles shed immediately before, and immediately after hibernation. Some peeling may be evident right before your turtle hibernates, but the real and extensive shedding will occur right after it emerges from hibernation, during which you might find it basking more often. This is completely natural and promotes both healing and growth.

Signs that your turtle's shell is peeling in a healthy way are:
Peeling scutes that are partially translucent and not too thick. These should look like the shell that they just came off of.
The peeling scutes will look like they are "lifting up" off the shell, and will generally come off on their own. Please do not try to physically force or remove the scutes yourself.
The scutes should be intact and whole, not coming off in parts.

Behavioral Characteristics of Turtles

Turtles are semi-terrestrial turtles that spend most of their time on land, and prefer to have a nearby source of water. Occasionally, they will soak in water and defecate in water, too. They do not, however, swim very well, so their soaking water should only be shallow and cleaned regularly to prevent contamination and infection from bacteria. It is therefore not advisable to house them in a water tank, or to provide them with a too-deep water bowl or dish in which they can possibly drown. Efficient water hygiene should be maintained, whether through water filtration or through simple daily changing of their water and regular cleaning of their water and food dishes.

Turtles come from a temperate climate, and their habitat usually consists of varying micro-environments with different temperatures and humidity levels among which they can move in order to regulate their body temperatures. Dehydration is a very real danger to them, so aside from plenty of shaded spots where they can take shelter from the sun, substrate deep enough that they can burrow into, readily available clean drinking water and a shallow water dish in which they can soak, they also need moderate levels of humidity in their environment. If you are keeping them in an indoor enclosure, it is best that this be equipped with substrate and plants that can help maintain humidity levels. Occasionally, you should mist the cage using clean, sprayed water.

Turtles are often shy and prefer privacy, but they can also be aggressive and territorial, particularly when you find different males in the same environment. For this reason, it is advisable to keep each turtle in their own separate enclosures. Not only does this prevent aggression and violence between different turtles, it also prevents unforeseen breeding and keeps down the chances of one sick turtle contaminating the rest.

Chapter 8. Breeding Your Turtles

The first thing you're going to need to know if you want to breed your turtle is how to tell the gender. It's fairly easy with turtles luckily.

The males will usually have red eyes and the females will have brown eyes. It really is that simple, so anyone can easily identify the gender of most turtles in seconds without even having to handle them.

The most reliable way to tell male from female, however, is to pick them up and examine their plastron (underbody shell). Males will have a concave area under the hinge. Another giveaway is the fact that males have longer tails than females.

Breeding Conditions

Turtles tend to mate immediately following or during rain because of the high humidity levels needed for the eggs to survive. They also tend to breed starting in the spring and going right through into autumn.

Mating Rituals and Process

Two mating turtles are fascinating to watch. Yes I am aware how strange that sounds! There are differences in the exact process between different species. Most will circle, bite and push each other about before mounting. Some may also pulsate their throats at different stages throughout the ritual.

The important part however is pretty much the same across the board. This is where the male's concave plastron comes in to play. It enables him to fit better against the female's shell and get into the proper position. After the male has inseminated the female, he may fall off backwards in a comical fashion. This however isn't funny for the males, who sometimes get stuck on their backs. This can result in getting stuck for a long time and eventually lead to death for the unfortunate male. If this happens, give him a helping hand.

Eggs

Turtle eggs are soft-shelled and oblong shaped. They are generally very small in size, at about 2–4 cm long. Clutch sizes vary depending on many factors and can range anywhere from just 1 egg up to 6 or 7.

Northern turtles tend to produce a larger amount of eggs per breeding cycle, whereas southern varieties of turtle have more cycles per year. Female turtles can actually lay fertile eggs for up to about four years after being inseminated by just one male.

Prior to laying their eggs, the females will dig a nest in the soil using their hind legs. She will then lay her eggs before covering the nest over to help keep in the humidity and maintain a constant temperature. The same female can lay several clutches in a single year.

Turtle eggs require a high level of humidity. If conditions are too dry, the eggs can actually dehydrate and collapse. A humidity level of over 80% is highly recommended at a temperature of about 80F (26 Celsius). If the conditions are right, your first turtle hatchlings will emerge from the eggs in roughly 70-80 days. There have been reports that suggest turtle eggs that are incubated at temperatures as low as 75F produce more males and those incubated at temperatures of about 85F produce more females. At about 80F you should get a nice mix.

Another tip is to disturb the eggs as little as possible. Unlike bird eggs, you should not turn turtle eggs. This can actually do a lot of damage and even kill the embryo. You can very carefully remove them and place them in an incubator in order to simulate the best conditions possible, just don't roll them and be as gentle as possible when digging them up and moving them.

Hatchling Care

When the hatchlings first emerge, they may take some time to fully exit the shell. This is normal, and some may even take a couple of days to fully emerge. You should not rush or try to coax them out, as they will still have the yolk sack attached to their underside. This is easily damaged and ruptured, which can easily prove fatal. The yolk sack will be quickly absorbed and they will be far safer to handle in just one or two days.

This yolk sack can sustain the hatchlings for at least a few weeks, so if they don't want to feed for a while, that's perfectly normal, just keep trying every day and eventually they will start to want to feed on insects.

They will also want to hide almost all of the time. This is probably due to the fact that in the wild they are too small to properly defend themselves, so they need to keep out of sight of predators as much as possible. Make sure they have plenty of hiding spots available to them.

The juvenile turtles should be kept separate from the adults until they are much older. The reason for this is because if the adults have any kind of parasitic infection, this can be passed on to the weaker juveniles, which can prove to be fatal.

Hatchlings and young turtles are also very sensitive to environmental and dietary factors. You must ensure their living conditions and dietary requirements are as optimal as possible to guarantee a high success rate.

As the weather gets colder you will notice that your turtles will eat less and less as time goes on. They will also move about less and generally be less active.

They may even hide away for days at a time. This could be in a hide out that you have provided for them, but they will probably also begin to dig holes in the ground and stay there for extended periods of time. They may well decide to make these holes their home for the winter.

We suggest adding extra dry leaves to the enclosure during this time, as this can act as an extra layer of insulation from the frost. If you have a mesh top to your enclosure, it is also a good idea to lay a sheet of wood or plastic over the top to prevent too much rain or snow getting in. It's also a great idea to cover the enclosure with something like old carpet weighed down with some rocks or bricks.

If you have any sick or underweight turtles, it is very important that you keep them inside over the winter. Only healthy animals will survive hibernation, so this is of vital importance. Other than that, just let them get on with it! In the wild they have to deal with hibernation and cold conditions, so as long as you don't live in a particularly cold part of the world and you cover the enclosure with carpet and add the dry leaves for insulation, they should be fine.

Mating between Turtles usually takes place throughout the spring and summer – after they come out of hibernation in March or early April. If you are keeping both a male and a female turtle as pets, then the possibility of their mating and breeding should be a reality you are aware of. If you do not wish them to breed, then you should do the responsible thing and keep them separate. Too many times, owners are just surprised when they see hatchlings emerging, not knowing how or when it happened. Like the breeding of most other pets, the breeding of turtles should be handled responsibly by the owners. The first consideration should always be the health, maturity, and suitability of the breeding pair.

Remember that breeding, egg formation and laying can consume much energy for both the male and the female. They should be of sufficient age, maturity and state of health to be able to undertake this task well. If at all possible, neither should they suffer from any illnesses or deformities that would make their breeding more difficult, or perhaps compromise the health and wellbeing of the offspring. Most breeders also recommend against the breeding of two related turtles because their offspring could suffer from weakness, deformities, or early death. If you do wish to breed your turtles, you should be responsible enough to think of the long-term results, including the care of the breeding pair and prospective parents, the care of the eggs and the hatchlings, and whether or not you will be able to find good homes for them later on. Be aware that certain states have laws against releasing captive bred turtles into the wild.

Selection and Care of the Breeding Pair
Ideally, you should choose adult male and female turtles of approximately similar size - approximately between 5-6 inches of carapace length, and between 7-10 years of age.
The female's fertility is largely dependent on her state of health, based on such general things as her diet and proper nutrition and being kept in a clean and low-stress environment. Keeping them in an outdoor enclosure will allow them to follow the natural seasonal changes to induce hibernation and turtle mating behavior, although some breeders do manage to induce these in indoor enclosures through the Refrigeration Method, which entails the preparation of a hibernacula kept at optimal temperatures. Either way, you should be able to check periodically on your turtle to make sure that they are kept safe, well insulated, and well-hydrated throughout their hibernation period. This natural process is often sufficient to induce turtle mating behavior.

The turtles should be in optimal health prior to breeding, which could take place for at least two months. Around spring or summer, as the turtles come out of hibernation, the males will have a strong urge to find a mate. You will probably observe some displays of their courtship ritual, including males circling the female, butting against her, and sometimes even biting her. Some males can often be quite aggressive, and will even try to bite the female's head and front legs when he mounts her. This is why it is so important to select turtles appropriately sized to each other.

The mating process itself is also pretty straightforward. When the female lowers her plastron, the male is then able to hook his feet beneath her carapace and they begin mating. The female will lock her carapace so that the male does not slide off during copulation, which can take place for about an hour or so.

The female's nesting and laying of eggs will take place around the warmer months of June or July, during which time you should have already provided your female with a solitary pen with a nesting site, ideally several choices of nesting sites among which she can make her selection. You can do this by providing rocks or large tree branches for cover, and a moist mix of sand and soft topsoil that is about 8 to 12 inches deep. This pen should be equipped in the same way that a turtle's main enclosure is equipped. The goal is to provide your female with the feeling of security and some privacy while also ensuring her optimal health and care.

Laying and Care of the Eggs

Around the time that the female is ready to lay her eggs, she will begin looking for an appropriate nesting spot. She will likely prefer a protected and private spot – usually near a tree or a rock. She will engage in digging her egg chamber using her back feet for several hours or until she has created a three-four inch deep receptacle for the eggs. Eggs usually average at 2-4, and are white, oval, with thin-walled and permeable shells. Once she is done laying her eggs, the female will cover them again with the soil she had displaced, packing the soil in place with her hind legs until you can hardly tell that the soil had been disturbed.

Eggs hatch approximately eighty days after being laid, but it could be difficult to pinpoint exactly when the eggs are actually laid. Females will bury the eggs after laying them, and it is strongly advised that you limit the checks on the enclosure because she would prefer solitude at this time. In fact, it is not advisable to disturb or move turtle eggs once they have been laid. Make sure to check on her (as opposed to looking for eggs) regularly all the same and don't be lax about changing her water, cleaning up her enclosure as best you can, and providing her with adequate food. Artificially incubating and hatching eggs requires expertise and experience, not to mention great expense, and is not something recommended for first time or novice turtle pet owners. If you do take the eggs away from the mother, it's quite likely that you won't produce any living hatchlings.

Care for the eggs will really be up to the mother after she has laid them, and your role in the process will be limited. Still, and particularly if your turtle is being kept in an outdoor enclosure, you might want to provide extra protection for the eggs. A wire mesh cover will help secure the eggs from other animals, including other turtles. It will also keep the hatchlings from escaping once they have hatched. While they will generally hatch around 80 days after being laid, the range of time can be anywhere from 70-90 days, depending on the prevailing temperature, which in turn determines how quickly the embryos will develop. If you find the soil or ground to be hard, you may want to water the ground around day 75. This helps the hatchlings dig their way out of the soil when they are ready to emerge.

If you find any eggs in odd places, unburied, or in the water dish, for instance, these are most likely unfertile eggs which the mother has knowingly discarded for this very reason.

Caring for the Hatchlings
In the wild, the mortality rate of turtle hatchlings is quite high. They are very susceptible to the elements, particularly in their first year, and they are considered prey by various animals such as rodents, ants, and raccoons. If the eggs have been kept in an outdoor enclosure until now, you might want to transfer them to an indoor enclosure during their first year. This is the time when it becomes

important for you to exercise care and protection over the hatchlings.

If you wish to keep them in an outdoor enclosure instead, make sure to provide the hatchlings with all the necessary protection they will need against probable predators and the elements; overexposure to the sun or to the rain could kill them just as easily as a frenzy of fire ants that might get into the enclosure. Provide them with areas of shade and a hide box, and ant bait could be used to keep fire ants from getting into the pens and feeding on the baby turtles. Practicing regular maintenance by cleaning out uneaten food and getting rid of waste also helps ensure minimal chances of ant incursions and bacteria or germs affecting the hatchlings.

If you have decided to move your hatchlings indoors, it is advisable to keep the hatchlings in separate tanks. If you do not wish to do this, it is advised that you feed them separately, as they can be quite aggressive during feeding time. If they also display aggression against littermates even outside of feeding time, then separating them from each other better ensures their survival as a whole. Their indoor tanks or enclosures usually consist of deep substrate which can be misted daily to maintain high humidity levels. The temperature should be maintained at around 82°F during the day, and around 75°F at night. You can maintain the tank's temperatures using an overhead lamp of 40-60 watts and/or a low wattage thermostat or heater. You can monitor the tank's temperature by the use of thermometers attached to the tank in several locations.

Clean the tank at least once or twice a month, depending on the conditions within the tank. Change the water daily, and make sure to clean or change beddings that contain the turtle's waste. Practicing good tank maintenance at this time will keep germs and bacteria at bay, and goes a long way in ensuring the good health and proper development and growth of your tiny turtle.

Provide the hatchlings with a hide where they can go if they wish to cool off a bit. Bring them outdoors at least once a week, providing them with filtered sunlight for at least an hour each time. Even then, you should always provide the hatchlings with a shaded or hiding place where they can retreat should the sun prove to be too intense for them. They should in no instance be left alone during this time. They could literally overheat under inappropriate conditions.

The recommended diet for a hatchling is one that is high in protein, at a ratio of around 80% protein and 20% plant matter. Small bugs, for instance, can give them much of their protein needs. Uneaten food should be cleaned out after an hour or these could attract bugs or insects, and possibly become a breeding ground for bacteria.

Exercise your best judgment in terms of caring for your hatchlings. This can consume much of your time and energy, but the difference in raising sick turtles to healthy ones makes all that effort worthwhile. Be observant of the hatchlings in your care, and learn to make adjustments accordingly depending on your observations. And of course, keep reading and asking questions – educate yourself and read as many available materials as you can find.

Chapter 9. Keeping Your Turtle Healthy

A lot of health issues that affect turtles are generally due to mistakes made by their owners, often as a result of poor advice. Turtles have been found to suffer far more health issues when kept in a vivarium indoors; this is also probably due to the increased chance of human error.

In this chapter we are going to go over some of the common mistakes and misconceptions that cause illness in turtles, along with some information on the common illnesses.

Environment

It's vital to ensure that your turtles are not exposed to high heat levels or dry conditions. While it's true that turtles are found in temperate regions in the wild, they are not found in extremely hot, tropical areas. Many owners do tend to treat turtles like a tropical reptile, so it's important to remember that they are not. Excessive heat and dryness is not good for them at all. If exposed to excessive heat, turtles can suffer from metabolic stress and kidney failure.

Wild Food

As I mentioned, when turtles are kept in an outdoor enclosure, they will be presented with a range of insects that they will more than happily feed on. The only problem with this is when the insects they are eating have come into contact with harmful chemicals.

You should never use any kind of pesticides in your garden if you are keeping turtles in an outdoor enclosure. Something that is especially problematic is slug pellets, as turtles love to eat slugs and snails. This can be extremely hazardous, so really do be careful with this.

Feeding techniques

Turtles eat in the water, which can make the tank filthy very fast. For this reason, turtle keepers may use a secondary tank as a feeding tank. The turtles are moved into the tank, fed, and then moved back to their main tank. The whole process takes about 30 minutes. However, moving from tank to tank won't work with some turtles. They'll become stressed and refuse to eat, and for those turtles, you'll have to feed them in their regular habitat and deal with the resulting mess. You can strain out larger bits of food the turtle leaves behind with an aquarium net, and the filtration system can clear the rest.

Aquarium Plants as Food

One of the most common questions many new turtle owners have is whether or not they can add plants to a turtle tank. The answer is a resounding yes, but it's important to explore both the benefits and drawbacks of adding plants to a turtle aquarium before you take the plunge, so to speak...

As a rule of thumb, it's best to wait until you're comfortable in your turtle care before you even consider adding live plants to a turtle habitat. Adding live plants signifies that you know how to care for your turtle each day and are willing to take your habitat to the next level.

However, if you already have experience with aquatic plants from a freshwater or marine fish tank, it may be easier to make the transition to add live plants to your turtle's habitat.

Pros of Live Plants in a Turtle Tank

1) Improved aesthetic and visual beauty to create a more natural habitat.
2) Provide places for turtles to hide and explore.
3) Provide food for turtles to eat.
4) Naturally filter ammonia and nitrates from the water to reduce algae growth.
5) Help oxygenate water to discourage harmful bacteria growth.

Cons of Live Plants in a Turtle Tank

1) Live plants may require substrate, which needs to be vacuumed and cared for at least twice a week to prevent pollution that could cause sickness in the tank.
2) Some plant species may be toxic to turtles.
3) Turtles that eat live plants could create a mess.
4) Turtles are prone to digging plants out by the roots, possibly out of boredom.

In general, the advantages outweigh the disadvantages when it comes to adding live plants to a turtle tank. But if you're brand new to the hobby, take some time to develop your experience in caring for turtles before adding live plants to a terrarium.
Many people add live plants to sand substrate, although it's difficult to keep clean. Sand is also quite dense, so it may be hard for water to circulate properly in the roots of the plants. Other pet shops recommend basic aquarium gravel, but this is not the best choice since sharp edges could injure your turtles, especially if they eat the gravel. Aquarium gravel also provides no nutrient value for plants. A recommended substrate for planted turtle tanks is clay-based gravel. It can be purchased for anywhere from $15 or £12 at a pet store. Clay-based gravel is stable, nontoxic, and provides nutrients for live plants in a turtle habitat.

Recommended Live Plants for Turtle Tanks
Consider the following criteria before adding any live plant to your turtle habitat:
a) Make sure the plant is non-toxic to turtles.
b) Make certain that the turtles won't be so attracted to the taste of the plant that they eat it before it can grow.
c) Check that the plant can thrive in a warm, low light environment like a turtle terrarium.

Once you have those important questions answered, there are quite a few popular, inexpensive live plants available at pet stores that you can add to your turtle habitat:

a) Waterweed, a.k.a. Egeria densa - This is a cheap plant that thrives in moderate environments, and it grows like a weed, just like the name suggests. It is also nutritious to turtles, but keep in mind that some turtle species are prone to eating too much of the plant and may create a mess in the terrarium. This plant is best kept in a tank with primarily carnivorous turtles that will eat it in moderation.

b) Java Fern, a.k.a. Microsorum pteropus - This is an inexpensive, popular aquarium plant that thrives in turtle terrariums. In its natural habitat, you may find it attached to rocks, driftwood, and other items that are submerged. The plant doesn't have roots per se, so you can't plant it directly into the substrate because it will most likely drift throughout the tank. The plant grows best when rooted between two rocks or tied to a piece of driftwood at the bottom of the tank.

c) Amazon Sword Plant, a.k.a. Echinodorus amazonicus - This is a hardy plant that requires ample light. It should not be planted in darker parts of a terrarium. Turtles are likely to nibble at the plant and may pull it up by the roots, but they normally won't overeat it. A Sword Plant has a root that can be planted directly into substrate; it can also be attached to a rock in order to develop roots.

d) Anubias Barteri, a.k.a. Anubias barteri - This plant is ideal for beginners; it grows slowly and is a suitable choice for a turtle terrarium. The plant is inexpensive and widely available at most pet supply stores. It thrives in low light and does not require a specific pH. However, the plant is bitter, so most turtles won't eat from it.

e) Hornwort, a.k.a. Ceratophyllum demersum - This plant can grow in low light but will thrive in moderate light. The plant grows quickly and helps to remove waste from water, but it may create clutter in the tank since the small branches are prone to breakage. The plant should be planted in the substrate with several stems tied together, or it will float throughout the tank. Turtles may eat the plant in moderation.

Turtles of the genus Terrapene are fairly hardy animals – though their state of health does depend, to a large extent, on you as their owner and how you keep them. They require specific care, and can be stressed by over-handling or when being moved into new surroundings. On the other hand, they can also be prone to certain illnesses and conditions - and most of the time, these are brought on by poor advice. This is why it is important that you do your research prior to, and during, your ownership, of a pet turtle. In many cases, appropriate environmental and dietary maintenance will address these problems successfully.

And yet, despite our best efforts, sometimes our pets can just get sick from time to time. Below are some of the more common health problems of turtles and recommended treatments.

Common Conditions Affecting Turtles
Below we take a closer look at some of the common conditions that turtles are prone to. If you are planning on keeping a turtle as a pet, or already have one, do your research and find a good turtle vet in your area, preferably one that has experience in dealing with this particular species. In fact, if you suspect your turtle of being sick, or notice any deviation in their usual behavior, bring them to a vet immediately. Try not to undertake any homemade treatments until after you have sought professional care and treatment.

Common conditions that can affect turtles include:

Swollen and Closed Eyes
Turtles originate from temperate (not tropical) environments, and they will not tolerate extreme heat or dryness. If there is not enough moisture in their environment, eye infections can be quite common. You may notice that your turtle's eyes are shut and won't open unless he is soaked in warm water. Another possible cause of eye infections is contaminated bathing or drinking water, or if its bedding is irritating to its eyes. Should the eyes be swollen enough that they become permanently closed, the turtle will not eat, thereby further compromising his health.

There are different ways by which you can maintain the humidity or moisture in your turtle's environment. Daily misting with water, readily available clean water that it can walk into any time it needs to, fixing a draft in the enclosure by which the turtle is drying out, and placing plants in the enclosure, will help maintain the humidity in your turtle's environment. Cedar shavings or cedar bark are not recommended because these contains oils that are toxic to most reptiles. Bedding such as shredded paper or corncob bedding can also be considered too absorbent for your turtle's environment.

If the eyes look sunken it, it could be a sign of severe dehydration. If the eyes are closed and puffy, on the other hand, and you notice a discharge from the eyes or nostrils, it could be a sign of respiratory infection or vitamin A deficiency. Consult your vet for proper diagnosis and treatment. Antibiotic eye ointment is usually quite effective in most cases.

Ear Abscesses

Ear abscesses are considered the number one health problem of captive turtles and this condition is usually caused by the same conditions that cause swollen eyes, such as poor turtle care that involves dirty water or water that is too cold, too much or too little humidity, a poor diet, or respiratory illnesses. Any of these conditions can allow bacteria to enter and infect a turtle's body.

While a turtle may develop an abscess anywhere underneath their skin, they are particularly susceptible to middle ear infections which can result in an abscess that can appear as large bulges on either side of the head, or what looks like a big bump on the side of the head, in the same area where the ears are. An ear abscess means that there is a swelling of the Tympanic membrane, and a cyst develops underneath it, growing worse as the infection does. On the other hand, bacterial abscesses in places other than the ear are often caused by puncture wounds, bite wounds, and other injuries. An ear abscess is very painful to your pet turtle, and requires professional treatment – an operation that requires either aspiration, or lancing, draining, and a lot of post-operative attention including antibiotics to kill off any remaining infection. It is also recommended that the site be left open to heal rather than being sutured after surgery, though take care to keep the area clean and covered, and protected from attacks by flies, other insects and animals. Otherwise, recurrences might be common.

Parasites
Turtles are semi-carnivorous, and so they are exposed to a wide range of parasites, as they eat many of the intermediate hosts. Practicing good and efficient hygiene will help keep the incidence of parasites down, but there will still be instances when your pet turtle might be attacked by either internal or external parasites. While all reptiles are prone to parasites, even in the wild, keeping them confined or in an enclosed space may increase the risks exponentially. That is why it is important to maintain the cleanliness of their surroundings – clean out fecal matter daily, and always clean out their water and food dishes. Needless to say, always wash your hands before and after handling any of your turtle's equipment.

Internal parasites are those which your turtle may ingest, such as worms (pinworms, hookworms, tape-worms, oxyurid and ascarid worms), protozoans that might be ingested when they eat contaminated foods or substrate, and other flagellate organisms.

Possible signs and symptoms that may indicate that your turtle may have internal parasites include:
1) Diarrhea
2) Constipation
3) Worms in the feces
4) Foaming mouth
5) Regurgitating food
6) Constipation

84

7) Lethargy
8) Lack of appetite
9) Weight loss
10) Dark green and smelly urine
11) Anorexia
12) Fluid retention

Should you notice any of these symptoms, it is advisable to bring your turtle to a vet. Generally, analysis of a stool sample will tell your vet whether internal parasites are indeed the problem. Deworming meds are usually prescribed. It is important, however, that Ivermectin and Piperazine should not be used since these could be toxic to your turtle.

External parasites, on the other hand, can include pests such as ticks, leaches, mites, mosquitoes, fire ants, fly larvae, and chiggers. These can usually take hold of your pet when they are housed in an outdoor pen, or if you add decorations or substrate to their enclosure without cleaning them first.

Treatment depends on which parasite you are dealing with. Many pests can simply be picked off or removed with a pair of tweezers, such as mites, leaches, and ticks. An infestation of fire ants need to be addressed differently, as these can kill your turtle by getting inside the shell once your pet tucks its head inside. The location of the ant nest should be located and exterminated if possible. Otherwise, bait traps can be laid so that the ants will not get inside your turtle's pen. Caution should always be exercised when dealing with chemicals of any kind, however, especially those your pet turtle might also be exposed to.

On the other hand, open wounds or injuries are susceptible to the laying of fly eggs and larvae – when these hatch, they will feed on the flesh as they grow. You will need professional treatment should this happen. There will be a swelling or small lumps on the skin from which pupate will emerge and fall off. A vet will need to cut open this lump and clean out the wound.

In any case, it is always advisable to seek professional assistance or to consult your veterinarian to help with the identification of the problem parasite, as well as the best way to remove any type of external or internal parasites. Proceeding recklessly will likely just worsen your turtle's condition.

Shell Rot

Also referred to as Septemic Cutaneous Ulcerative Disease (SCUD), this happens when an open wound or other injury becomes infected by a fungus or bacteria, or it can happen due to a filthy environment. Malnutrition can be a predisposing factor. When shell rot takes place, either the upper shell or the lower shell can suffer erosion. While this happens more often among aquatic turtles, this can also happen with land species like turtles.

The primary way of preventing shell rot is by keeping the turtle's enclosure clean. The build-up of fungus inside the confined space can usually be attributed to poor water quality. A soft, discolored shell that may or may not smell rotten is a sign of wet rot. Dry rot, on the other hand, is seen through a flaky, pitted shell with whitish patches. It is imperative that you change your turtle's water often. This is true even if the water still seems clear and clean. Filters should be cleaned regularly using cool water. Feces and all uneaten food should be removed as soon as possible. Your turtle should have a readily accessible dry area where it can bask and dry their shell when needed. The important thing is to minimize the possible places where bacteria or fungus can take hold and thrive.

If you suspect your turtle of having shell rot, bring him to your vet immediately. Shell rot needs to be treated immediately before it gets any worse, and your vet will work on removing the rotten parts while prescribing antibiotics to fight infection. Should their skin also be affected by the fungus, a salt bath for the next 4-5 days can help.

Afterwards, your turtle should be kept dry with only a limited time in the water each day. This keeps the infection from spreading. The short soaking time each day would keep your turtle from becoming dehydrated. Afterwards, the conditions which led to the rot in the first place need to be addressed: regularly changed clean water, with a dry area where your turtle can bask and dry out their shell is important. Otherwise, shell rot can keep coming back. If it becomes a systemic infection, it can take a very long time to heal, not to mention that severe shell rot can eventually work its way into your turtle's blood and bones. The owner should be vigilant in preventing this from happening in the first place, or from recurring if it should happen.

Respiratory Infection
This is another possible result of poor environmental conditions, typically of enclosures that are kept too dry or too damp, sometimes too cold. Remember that turtles hail from a temperate environment. Poor care can cause a runny nose and swollen eyes, and they will not necessarily develop into an infection unless the condition is prolonged. When this happens, the turtle's condition can worsen into an actual infection.

Some of the earlier signs that should alert you that something is wrong include open-mouthed breathing, mucous coming from the mouth, lack of appetite, and lethargy. When it becomes a full-blown infection, you'll notice your turtle swimming lopsided, breathing with a gaping motion or with raspy or wheezing sounds, and that they are basking more often than usual while at the same time showing difficulty breathing. Sometimes, you may even see discharge or bubbles forming from their nose or eyes.

Most vets will prescribe antibiotics, and this should do the trick provided the conditions that led to the development of this condition in the first place are corrected.

Metabolic Bone Disease (MBD)

Metabolic Bone Disease or MBD, also sometimes called nutritional secondary hyperarathyroidism, is the result of a variety of ongoing environmental factors, including poor diet, lack of needed vitamins and minerals such as Vitamin D, a poor calcium and phosphorous ratio, lack of exercise, too much protein and fat, poor lighting, and low humidity.

When MBD strikes a young turtle, their growth and development is also compromised, and various deformities and poor body structure is the result: a soft or malformed shell and bones, stacked or raised scutes on the carapace, overgrown or parrot-like beaks, odd curvature in the nails, splayed legs, shells that curve upward like saddles, thickened shells, and thin and deformed legs. Because of the malformation of their legs and nails, they will also have difficulty walking.

MBD is the result of long-term exposure to poor conditions, and the best way to address it is through prevention: do your research properly on the proper housing conditions for your turtle. Provide them with a clean environment, a nutritious diet with a good supply of calcium and Vitamin D, appropriate lighting, plenty of exercise and the proper amounts of humidity.

This is a slow-growing condition, which means that it is not always easy to catch in the beginning. It is recommended that as soon as you notice any shell deformity, you should take a second look at their diet and living conditions to assess whether they are lacking in calcium, vitamin D, or exposure to full spectrum sunlight, that helps in the building of strong bones. Bring them to a vet for a professional diagnosis, and a consultation regarding changes you are planning on making. Make adjustments as are necessary. If this condition goes untreated for a long time, it will eventually result in the turtle's death.

Transmission to humans

When it comes to health issues, it isn't just the health of your turtle that you have to take care of, but also your own health and the health of the rest of your family or household. This is because reptiles such as the turtle can be carriers of bacteria that, while it may not make the turtle sick, can have a very different effect on humans. Reptiles, for instance, may carry salmonella which can cause salmonellosis in humans. This is a serious illness that can lead to diarrhea and vomiting in humans, and more severe symptoms in humans with compromised immune systems.

It is always best to practice good hygiene when dealing with pet animals.

Below are some practical tips you can practice to help prevent any incidences of possible disease transmission from animals to humans:

It is best to assume that your pet turtle carries the salmonella bacteria until after you've had him tested and cleared by a vet. Make this a yearly checkup with your vet to ensure your pet's continued good health and to check for possible illnesses, bacteria, or other diseases.

Young children, particularly those younger than 5, and people with compromised immune systems are the ones most at risk. If they are part of your household, then perhaps a turtle is not the best pet for you to keep. If you already do have a turtle at home, the young children and those with compromised immune systems should not be allowed to touch your turtle.

To help prevent the possible spread of bacteria or infection, always be meticulous in washing and cleaning your hands after handling your pet turtle, or any part of their tools, equipment, or habitat.

Your turtle should not be allowed to roam freely in your house. If you use any household items or fixtures, like a sink or a tub to soak your turtle, be sure to disinfect the sink or tub afterwards. Never clean any of your turtle's equipment and items in or near places where you prepare food. Use outdoor wash pans and faucets as much as possible, and clean and disinfect these afterwards. Keep your turtle's enclosure or habitat clean, and make sure you dispose properly of any waste afterwards.

If you are going to allow young kids to touch or handle the turtle, supervise the children closely. Make sure that they do not kiss the turtle or place their hands or fingers into their mouths. Afterwards, supervise the child as they wash their hands thoroughly.

Conclusion

Getting a pet is always a very important decision that one should make only when you are ready to take up the responsibility and you are aware of what having a pet will entail. The type of turtle, the time and money involved in getting one, the needs and requirement of feeding a turtle and giving it the right environment which is much required for its health and growth are the various factors you should consider before purchasing this innocent creature. Before you go out and decide to buy one, give yourself some time to introspect and ask yourself important questions. The most important one is the matter of commitment; if you are sure about committing to the well-being and health of having a turtle.

Turtles and tortoises being a very complex set of reptiles, they have a very different specialized set of needs. These reptiles can die prematurely if the owner doesn't provide them with their specialized needs. The quality of life they have becomes poor in such cases. In contrast to this, there are certain turtle or tortoise owners who provide excellent conditions for their captivity.

First you need to realize whether you need a turtle or a tortoise, because the requirements and environment vary from one species to another. Second important question is why we need to buy a pet turtle or tortoise, because it may be a commitment of lifetime if they get to outlive you. The welfare of the animal should be the primary focus while making such decisions.

CPSIA information can be obtained
at www.ICGtesting.com
Printed in the USA
LVOW10s1817031117
554902LV00010B/749/P